A Journey to Healthy Living

FULFILLING THE CALL ON YOUR LIFE

Dr. Teresa S. Johnson

authorHOUSE®

AuthorHouse™
1663 Liberty Drive
Bloomington, IN 47403
www.authorhouse.com
Phone: 1 (800) 839-8640

Published by AuthorHouse 12/21/2015

ISBN: 978-1-5049-6978-9 (sc)
ISBN: 978-1-5049-6959-8 (hc)
ISBN: 978-1-5049-6979-6 (e)

Library of Congress Control Number: 2015921141

Print information available on the last page.

Any people depicted in stock imagery provided by Thinkstock are models, and such images are being used for illustrative purposes only. Certain stock imagery © Thinkstock.

This book is printed on acid-free paper.

All scripture references found throughout the book are listed in the Notes section in the back of the book.

REAPERS for Christ Ministries
PO Box 4605
Midlothian, Virginia 23112

Email: reapersforchristministries@yahoo.com
Website: http://www.reapersforchristministries.org
To donate through the Combined Federal Campaign (CFC) #35461 log onto www.cfcnca.org

Editors:
Ericka N. Johnson
Roxanne Ledbetter

Contents

Dedication

I wrote this book because so many people go through life uttering the words, "I don't know what my purpose is." They truly act as if they don't have a clue what they are supposed to be doing with their lives. I too have been there. But when you know that what you are doing is what you were created to do, life is much more fulfilling. In short, we were all created to love God and do what He says. I say do what you do consistently and whole heartedly and in all your doing, "Please God!"

This book is dedicated to the following:

To those who are God conscious. To those who are searching for the things of God, I am confident you will find your way just as I am discovering my way. The key is to please God.

Acknowledgments

To My Heavenly Father, Alpha and Omega:

I thank God for all the challenges, struggles as well as good times, for without them I would not be on the path I am on today. Life can be hard at times, but when you know why you do what you do, and when you are assured that you are on the right track with God, life is much simpler. Through every trial, tribulation, all the grief, despair, anger, frustration along with the abundance of blessings, favor and the Grace of God, I would not trade my life. Every one bears a cross. Everyone goes through highs and lows. But through it all, God has been my source, strength, shield and protection. Without God I would not be writing today, I would be in some corner totally broken.

To my husband, Eric:

We have traveled this journey a long time, but what I am grateful for is that we are on the same path and enjoying the ride together. I am happy that God gave me you to travel with.

To my daughter, Ericka:

There has never been a time when I haven't appreciated having you in my life. You have been the most inspirational, encouraging, uplifting, nonjudgmental person I know. I am so grateful to God to have you. I pray life's journey fulfills you every day.

To my parents and siblings:

(Clarence and Aletha Streat), Clarence Streat, Jr., Sheila Streat, Douglas Streat, Fredric Streat (deceased), Minister Donnel Streat, Michael Streat, Tameka Streat, and Kim Henderson

We're all destined for greatness. I pray we all reach that greatness. Each of us has gone through things that some will never experience, but the Grace of God has kept us individually and collectively. Continue traveling on your journey until your mission is completed.

Minister Donnel: Thank you for serving as a co-laborer in the ministry and in our family. I cherish our discussions about the things of God. You represent the kingdom well.

To REAPERS For Christ/REAPERS For Christ Ministries:

Regardless to which way your life turns, just know that God is in charge of your destiny. He charts your course. Go through life with joy, peace and contentment in the things of God.

To my Spiritual Covering:

Bishop Daniel Robertson, Jr., and Co-Pastor Elena Robertson, Mt. Gilead Full Gospel International Ministries, Richmond, Virginia

It is a blessing to be around those who understand that we all must make the best of our journey. We all must cross the finish line with Excellency with the ultimate goal being to bring God Glory.

To my Mentor:

Pastor Bessie "Tish" Taylor Jett, Church
without Walls, Huntly, Virginia

Thank you for standing on the side lines, running along beside me, and cheering me on when nearing the finish line in many areas of my life. I appreciate you. You have been there since the beginning of me stepping out into ministry, even while I was discovering who I am in Christ and what I am supposed to be doing.

To the Reader:

You cannot go through life without others in your circle or even in your corner. This journey has so many different phases. Family is most definitely what keeps you going, but outside of them there needs to be special people along the way. Get some pick me uppers in your circle.

To My Special Friends, Ethel and Roxanne:

Many have come into my life, many have added something to my life, but you two have come into my heart. It's good to have a mature support system, and people who are invested in friendships. The two of you have been with me throughout much of my journey and you have been consistent.

Ethel Barnes you have been a blessing to me and have taught me much about the survival of marriage, tough decisions, standing your ground, remaining positive, and what a true friend looks like. I love you dearly.

Roxanne Ledbetter you have been a true friend to me, and I appreciate your supportive and genuine spirit. Thank you for being a blessing to me in multiple ways. You have stood with me for years and for that I say thank you.

To a devoted Intercessor:

Minister Nancine Dreon, thank you for continuously interceding on my behalf even before I asked and regardless to the topic. I appreciate you. I know it takes a special person to connect with me personally in prayer, but you have done that because of your connection to God.

Chapter One

The Plan

"I know what I'm doing"

When God allows you to see glimpses of your future, it's priceless. It motivates you to work even harder with the little you know. It gives you strength to continue running the race. It's uplifting because you can see where He is taking you even if you don't see the entire route mapped out before you. Having the privilege of seeing what God decides to share with you not only shows you how He sees you, but it shows the level of trust He has for you. If you saw the "you" that God knows, you would totally be in awe. If God allowed you to see what you will be doing in your future, you would be baffled.

With the limited sight that I have, it is enough to provoke me to continue running the race set before me with enthusiasm. There is no way I could ever turn back or quit after being included in all I have been privy to. God has entrusted me with information pertaining to my present and my future, and it sure looks good and sounds good to me. More than anything, I am excited and honored to have the details that God has chosen to share with me about my life. God is truly gracious.

Ultimately, seeing some of where God is taking you should give you some indication of whom you really are. Stop and think about it. The places God shows you have to wow you when you reflect on where you are right now. It's utterly amazing to see some of what God has for you, and it's equally exciting to see some of where God is taking you. He doesn't show you these things so that you can think more highly of yourself than you ought to, yet He doesn't want you to think any less of yourself than you ought to either.

The glimpses you see are designed to provide you with greater confidence in "you." We really do have more going for ourselves than we give credit. The glimpses increase your vision. You have to begin to see yourself as God sees you. Sometimes we focus on where we are and what we don't have, while God focuses on where we're going and what we do have. Those glimpses are strategically set forth to allow you to rest in your full authority now because of the authority you were ordained to walk in later.

The Route . . .

> ➤ *Jeremiah 6:16 NLT, This is what the Lord says: "Stop at the crossroads and look around. Ask for the old godly way, and walk in it. Travel its path, and you will find rest for your souls. But you reply, 'No, that's not the road we want!'*

Only God knows where He is taking you and where you are going. You may not always see what He sees, but you can always trust what He sees. As long as you have a connection with God, you have a commitment from God full of certainty. Jesus said in **John 14:1-6 KJV, "Let not your hearts be troubled: ye believe in God, also believe in me. In my Father's house are many mansions: if it were not so, I would have told you. I go to prepare a place for you. And if I go and prepare a place for you, I will come again, and receive you unto myself; that where I am, there ye may be also. And whither I go ye know, and the way ye know.**

Thomas said unto him, Lord, we know not whither thou goest; and how can we know the way? Jesus saith unto him, I am the way, the truth, and the life; no man cometh unto the Father, but by me." Jesus has the full plan, and the mapped out route we are to take along our journey. This detailed plan is one we can follow blind folded.

There is security in knowing that God holds every detail of the plan for you. The vision He shares is a result of all of the intricate details of the plan He has intertwined together. His plan is the best fit for your life. Because you were custom made, the plan for your life cannot be duplicated. It doesn't fit your cousin, or your best friend. It was designed for you. That's why it's important to stay in your lane, and be the unique you that God created you to be.

Some people may not understand your makeup and may set out to realign you. Some may try to make adjustments within you. Some may be tempted to tweak you just a little, but it's not their place to adjust, tweak or realign you. Your molding, shaping and purging comes from God. You cannot make a person become who you want them to become. You cannot impose upon a person what you will for them to do. God is the master of every masterpiece. He wills an individual to do a thing. Paul says in **Philippians 2:13 NIV, "For it is God who works in you to will and to act in order to fulfill his good purpose."**

Thankfully, as you acknowledge that God knows exactly what He is doing with your life and in your life, you will be able to love the life you live. God's plan is not outdated; it's not a fly by night plan. It was well thought out, and strategically designed to sheer perfection. Paul encourages us in **Ephesians 2:10 NLT, "For we are God's masterpiece. He has created us anew in Christ Jesus, so we can do the good things he planned for us long ago."** God prepared in advance good works for you to do. The fact that He is letting you in on the plan early on signifies that He wants to make sure His plan gets you to the best and most successful you. His way is the perfect way. His direction is the most secure direction.

The Prophet **Jeremiah** shares in **Chapter 29, verse 11, NIV, "For I know the plans I have for you, declares the LORD, plans to prosper you and not to harm you, plans to give you hope and a future."** God wants to get you to your expected end. He has high expectations for you. His expectations are well within your reach.

Oftentimes we reach for goals, and strive to live out our plan for our lives, but when we fall short of reaching our goals and our plan fails, anxiety and discouragement set in. We tend to get desperate and that desperation takes us out of sync because we're trying to make things happen. When your goals fall within the scope of God's plan, they will be accomplished. You don't have to be anxious for anything. Paul admonishes us in **Philippians 4:6 NIV, "Do not be anxious about anything, but in every situation, by prayer and petition, with thanksgiving, present your requests to God."**

Since God knows the plan, allow God to show you how to work the plan. When He gives you the vision, certainly run with it, but don't take off running so fast that you leave Him holding the details of the vision. Be sure you understand the message so that when you run with it, you are running with the correct message. Make sure you read the vision God gives you clearly. The Prophet **Habakkuk** recorded his conversation with the Lord in **Chapter 2 verses 2-3 NLT, "Then the LORD said to me, Write my answer plainly on tablets, so that a runner can carry the correct message to others. This vision is for a future time. It describes the end, and it will be fulfilled. If it seems slow in coming, wait patiently, for it will surely take place. It will not be delayed."**

Some people struggle with impatience. They may not mind the direction of the plan God has, but they grow weary in following the plan. Impatience can sometimes cause you to make snap decisions. For some, impatience holds a stiff penalty. When some don't see progress as fast as they want it, their actions can exhibit distrust. Distrust can breed discouragement causing the individual to run the risk of straying from the path God has for them.

We cannot be naïve to the fact that just as obedience causes manifestations, disobedience can cause delay in the manifestation of God's plan. When you have been given instruction for your life, and you are well within the plan God designed for your life, you will definitely experience more highs. The same is true when you operate in disobedience, you will experience more lows.

Obedience is always good, but unfortunately on the way to where God is taking you, you run into other people trying to figure out the plan for their lives; People who haven't considered the plan for their lives; or people who don't understand that there is a plan for their lives. The thing to remember is, though my plan may resemble your plan; it's not your plan.

I may be able to provide insight from the wisdom of working through my own plan, but I am not your source. I may have advanced in working through the stages of my plan, but I don't have all the answers. The masterplan comes from the Master who created the blueprint of the plan. Though God gives me insight and wisdom, and allows me to prophesy to you about your plan, I have limited information. Why seek limited information when you can go directly to the Master and receive the clear vision. You should desire to receive the details of the plan for your personal life from God. And if the information you receive is limited, let it be because God has limitations on it.

I highlight the importance of seeking God because some people really don't know God. They know what people tell them about God. They go to people to get answers, and solutions. After they get the answers they're good until the next problem arises. What they are getting is good information but it is also second hand information. That's all good and dandy when you're a babe in Christ, but once you reach maturity and are able to digest meat, you should crave meat.

If you purchase beef, you have the option to choose, USDA Prime, Choice or Select. A quality grade has tenderness, juiciness, and flavor. In beef, yield grades estimate the amount of boneless, closely trimmed retail cuts from the high-value parts of the carcass, the round, loin, rib, and chuck. The expected USDA Yield Grade with the highest percentage of boneless, closely trimmed retail cut is rated 1. This means you cut the fat, and get straight to the meat.

You don't purchase the lowest quality and grade of meat if you don't have to. In other words, when you constantly go through people to get to God, it is equivalent to USDA Select, yield grade 5, cutting through the fat to get to the meat. The middle man is good for a season, but sooner or later you will find yourself in a situation where you cannot call on anyone but God. Learn to feed yourself daily. You will eat better than ever. Don't let Sundays and midweek services become your only meals. Don't allow others to be your only access or connection to God. He wants to hear your voice.

God does not want to be separated from you. He desires to commune with you daily. Regardless to what stage you are in right now with your walk with God, if you want to learn how to receive from Him, He will honor that. Spending time with Him will bring clarity, direction and revelation.

Too many people are people seekers instead of God seekers. When you learn to go to God with your desires, questions, concerns, needs and wants, fulfillment will take place. Yes, God uses Apostles, Bishops, Pastors, Prophets, Evangelists, and people in general, but those people regardless to titles do not replace God.

Without the leading of the Holy Spirit, the anointing of God, or revelation from God, none of those people would have an answer or even a partial answer to your problem or question. God certainly uses people to assist others, to inspire and encourage others, and to offer hope to others, but first and foremost you should seek out the one who gave so much to those attempting to assist, inspire, encourage, or offer hope.

The scripture provides a prerequisite for getting what you need. **Matthew 6:33 NLT says, "Seek the Kingdom of God above all else, and live righteously, and he will give you everything you need."** It's all about God. Go after God. But whatever you do, don't chase people and status. You do know that some people follow pastors closer than they follow God. Paul says in **1 Corinthians 11:1 NIV, "Follow my example, as I follow the example of Christ."** Man may mean well but may not always do well. God will always operate in truth.

Explore God's plan first and see if your desired plan falls within His plan. If it doesn't, your plan wasn't a good plan to begin with. If you insist your plan was good, and it doesn't fall within God's plan, understand it was not the best plan for you. Everything that feels good to you is not good for you. Just as some things that may appear as skepticism turns into certainty or sureness. God's plan may not feel good to you starting off, but in the end it can literally save your life.

The Detour . . .

> *Exodus 13:17-18 NLT, "When Pharaoh finally let the people go, God did not lead them along the main road that runs through Philistine territory, even though that was the shortest route to the Promised Land. God said, "If the people are faced with a battle, they might change their minds and return to Egypt." So God led them in a roundabout way through the wilderness toward the Red Sea. Thus the Israelites left Egypt like an army ready for battle."*

Stubborn people suffer an array of consequences. I was very stubborn in my immature state. But I quickly learned if you continue being obstinate, you will continue stumbling through life instead of coasting. **Proverbs 16:9 NLT says, "We can make our plans, but the Lord determines our steps."** If you are not walking God's way, you could be walking in circles for years and not even realize it.

No matter how you look at it, God holds the master plan. I have learned that you can paint a clear picture for some people, yet they are too stubborn to admit what they see or act on what they see. I have also experienced life whereas, when I listened and accepted what I saw, it was easier and much more productive.

Remember, the Israelites wandered through the wilderness for 40 years in what could have taken 11 days **(Joshua 5:6 NLT)**. I have been in positions that I should not have been in. I have stayed in ruts longer than I wanted to, but I quickly learned. Some people say experience is the best teacher. I prefer to learn from your mistakes. I want to alleviate as much pain and suffering as I possibly can from my life.

I have heard it said when you look in the mirror, if you don't like what you see, change it. I have also heard it said, instead of focusing on what you see in the mirror, focus on looking up. Of course, that means looking up to God. His opinion is most critical.

Disobedience doesn't look good on anyone, but it is a choice. I know too much about God to outright disobey Him. He has gotten me through much, and kept me from more than enough. I show my gratitude by listening and obeying. Some things I just cannot do because of my reverence for God. And the things that I did do, I regret doing because it hurt God.

When I think about the direction my life is headed in, outside of God's grace and mercy, I know the positive direction is primarily due to me choosing to make better decisions. I read the manual that was inspired by God, and I apply the principles. I'm not ashamed to say, I want God to tell me what to do and how to do it. He doesn't want hand puppets, but I will be His puppet. I'm at the stage of, just lay out the instructions for me and I shall follow them.

Have you ever given someone directions to your house, and it took them forever to get there because they decided to go the way they wanted to go instead? Or maybe they turned around because they got lost. Some people just don't like following instructions.

I used the analogy of relating to Jesus knowing the way to God, to a homeowner knowing the way to his or her house. Here's an example: You know your address. You know where your house is located. You know the route to get there. As you get close to your house, there may be one road that leads you straight to your house. Along comes someone who doesn't know your address. He or she doesn't know where your house is located. They do not know the fastest route to take to get there. Nor do they know the direct road that leads straight to your house.

However, if you give them the address, and specific details as to the main road to take, provide some landmarks, maybe even shortcuts, they will end up at your house. It is a known fact that you must provide clear directions if you want the assurance that the individual will find your house. So it is with God. Jesus knows the way to God. He is the way to God. Jesus knows you cannot get to God's house without Him taking you, showing you, or telling you how to get there. The instructions and directions are clear if we would only follow.

Jesus knows you cannot gain entry or access to God without Him being involved. He provides landmarks (Confession Avenue, Faith Lane, Acceptance Boulevard, Jesus Path, and God Road.) With that being said, if you miss the landmarks, and don't follow Jesus' instructions or directions, you are not going to make it to God's house. If you are determined to be stubborn and try to get to God's house your way, you will end up at a dead end.

The Connection . . .

> ➤ *1 John 1:1-4 NLT, "We proclaim to you the one who existed from the beginning, whom we have heard and seen. We saw him with our own eyes and touched him with our own hands. He is the Word of life. This one who is life itself was revealed to us, and we have seen him. And now we testify and proclaim to you that he is the one who is eternal life. He was with the Father, and then he was revealed to us. We proclaim to you what we ourselves have actually seen and heard so that you may have fellowship with us. And our fellowship is with the*

> *Father and with his Son, Jesus Christ. We are writing*
> *these things so that you may fully share our joy."*

The plan God has for you comes with connectors: God, Jesus, the Holy Spirit, and it involves you. Without any of these connectors, there is no plan worth carrying out. There is no successful, lasting, effective plan. God the Father, God the Son, and God the Holy Spirit are necessities for the plan called life. God provides instructions. Jesus paved the way for us to carry out the instructions, and the Holy Spirit helps us to live out the instructions.

It's something to behold when you think about all that took place to give us access to God. Jesus prayed in **John 17:1-5 NIV, "Father, the hour has come. Glorify your Son, that your Son may glorify you. For you granted him authority over all people that he might give eternal life to all those you have given him. Now this is eternal life: that they may know you, the only true God, and Jesus Christ whom you have sent. I have brought you glory on earth by finishing the work you gave me to do. And now, Father, glorify me in your presence with the glory I had with you before the world began."** Hearing Jesus pray to the Father is extremely emotional. The love exudes from Him.

The plan God had for Jesus was the greatest plan we will ever be allowed to participate in. We get to be included because we are His followers. Discipleship has its benefits. Jesus is definitely committed to us. He prayed for His disciples in **John 17:6-12 NIV, "I have revealed you to those whom you gave me out of the world. They were yours; you gave them to me and they have obeyed your word. Now they know that everything you have given me comes from you. For I gave them the words you gave me and they accepted them. They knew with certainty that I came from you, and they believed that you sent me.**

I pray for them. I am not praying for the world, but for those you have given me, for they are yours. All I have is yours, and all you have is mine. And glory has come to me through them. I will remain in the world no longer, but they are still in the world, and I am coming to you. Holy Father, protect them by the power of your name, the name you gave me, so that they may be one as we are one. While I was with them, I protected them and kept them

safe by that name you gave me. None has been lost except the one doomed to destruction so that Scripture would be fulfilled."

The prayer may be lengthy, but when Jesus is praying for us, and doing so in such a moving way, who dares to have the audacity to count the seconds until He is done. With a prayer like that, everyone under the reading of my writing should be affirmed. When the highs and lows of life hits, the highs should bring peace on the mountain and the lows should bring peace in the valley.

Jesus continued praying in **John 17:13-19 NIV, "I am coming to you now, but I say these things while I am still in the world, so that they may have the full measure of my joy within them. I have given them your word and the world has hated them, for they are not of the world any more than I am of the world. My prayer is not that you take them out of the world but that you protect them from the evil one. They are not of the world, even as I am not of it. Sanctify them by the truth; your word is truth. As you sent me into the world, I have sent them into the world. For them I sanctify myself, that they too may be truly sanctified."** Is this encouraging or what?

We all know life has highs and lows. Some, we bring upon ourselves and some we have no control over. The key to remember is even in the lows, you can trust the hand of God. You can always trust in the plan created by God. He took into consideration the highs and the lows you would experience along the way of life. He foresees what you cannot see. Look at who we have on our side. God's protection is permanent.

Jesus prays in **John 17:24-26 NIV, "Father, I want those you have given me to be with me where I am, and to see my glory, the glory you have given me because you loved me before the creation of the world. Righteous Father, though the world does not know you, I know you, and they know you that you have sent me. I have made you known to them, and will continue to make you known in order that the love you have for me may be in them and that I myself may be in them."** I can say with certainty, I know God, and I will continue to make Him known. I got Jesus down on the inside of me for sure.

I recall my daughter telling me I was obsessed with God and I am. There's more that I want to know about Him, but I'm happy with what I do know. Years ago, I shared a problem I was going through with one of my brothers and I commented, you know I must have Jesus. He responded, "You must have Jesus or you're crazy." Certainly, I'm peculiar but not crazy. I was merely operating under the full degree of God's love in a dark situation.

Jesus knew we would experience the evil one and He made provisions to help us through each encounter. Whatever you go through, knowing that God holds you and the plan He has for you in the palm of His hands is very comforting. David said in **Psalm 119:50 NIV, "My comfort in my suffering is this: Your promise preserves my life."** Because of Jesus, we have been preserved. His prayers back then are still in effect today.

It is evident that everyone goes through forms of suffering at some point or another. It is definite that God makes promises to all of His children and addresses every form of suffering. It is obvious that some people take advantage of the promises God provides, while others doubt He will or can fulfill His promises. But the truth of the matter is, everything will eventually become as water under the bridge.

David found the solution that comforted him. For David, the promise of God was enough. It sustained him. The promise provided nourishment for David. It was life changing in that it allowed him to continue on the path of righteousness, trusting in the Word of God to keep him through every situation. Sure, David remembered the negative experiences and the downtrodden state he was once in, but the blessings and favor of God outweighed the negative. What it came down to was David realized that challenges only appeared impossible when God was left out of the equation. It is true, David did not know the entire plan for his life, but he trusted the entire plan.

In your life, "Do what you know to do with what you know." And for the part of the plan that you do not know, trust God to do what He knows to do. Put your hope in God's Word. Keep His Word at the forefront of your heart. His word can prevent other stuff from filtering into your heart. I don't know about you, but I don't worry half as much when I focus on who God is.

Isaiah 49:16 ESV says, "Behold, I have engraved you on the palms of my hands; your walls are continually before me." God will never forget you. God's plan keeps you on track, but you must remain focused and determined. In my own life, in the midst of turmoil where I believe confusion thrives, and nonsense lurks, I found that God was still actively working for my good. He cared about what concerned me, even what others may have considered petty. It was my petty stuff and God cared so much for me that when something affected me, it mattered to Him.

It's good to have a Father who comes in the twinkling of an eye to give you a word to stand on. It's good to have a Father you can rely on who also backs His Word. When you have a Father who make promises to you and those promises actually comes to pass, it does something to your faith. It takes you from faith to knowing, and from knowing to increased faith. It's wonderful to have a Father who can calm your spirit in the midst of a storm. A heavenly Father can be so much to you on so many levels.

While Jesus is the Way, the Truth, and The Life, He made the Father known to us. Jesus came so that we might have Life. The abundant life on earth, as well as life everlasting with the Father is something to be desired. Jesus wants to give you a rich and satisfying life. It's a double dose of goodness, life on earth is good, and life after earth is good. I have tasted the abundance on earth and I have high expectations of the great life after earth. God has demonstrated He is everything we need or will ever need.

Jesus didn't come to condemn the world. **John 3:17 AMP says, "For God did not send the Son into the world in order to judge (to reject, to condemn, to pass sentence on) the world, but that the world might find salvation and be made safe and sound through Him."** Unfortunately, evil was in the world when Jesus got here. As a result, a penalty was put in place to combat evil. Jesus destroys the work of the evil one.

John 3:19-20 AMP says, "The basis of the judgment (indictment, the test by which men are judged, the ground for the sentence) lies in this: the Light has come into the world, and people have loved the darkness rather than and more than the Light, for their works (deeds) were evil. For every wrongdoer

hates (loathes, detests) the Light, and will not come out into the Light but shrinks from it, lest his works (his deeds, his activities, his conduct) be exposed and reproved." You don't have to participate in darkness.

Jesus learned active, special obedience through what He suffered. And His completed experience is what made Him perfectly equipped to carry out the work of God. You can turn your suffering into strengths. Your experiences are valuable to more than just you. Learn from your trials. Allow tribulation to push you into your divine call.

The Sideshow Distractions . . .

> *1 Corinthians 7:35 NLT, "I am saying this for your benefit, not to place restrictions on you. I want you to do whatever will help you serve the Lord best, with as few distractions as possible."*

No matter how good life is, there is always a sideshow distraction. **Proverbs 4:25-27 MSG says "Keep your eyes straight ahead; ignore all sideshow distractions. Watch your step, and the road will stretch out smooth before you. Look neither right nor left; leave evil in the dust."** You have to continue to look straight ahead, fixing your eyes on what's ahead. You have to mark a straight path for your feet, staying on the safe path.

Don't let the noise of the world keep you from hearing the voice of God. If you are human, then you know there's an adversary who wants to oppose you by any means necessary. While you cannot focus on the adversary, it is good to recognize his tactics. The enemy knows you have victory, but sometimes it's hard for you to see that you have victory. You cannot afford to get sidetracked; you must keep your feet from following evil. Remember, God controls your destiny and He will see you through.

The enemy clearly sought to destroy me time and time again. But he cannot succeed. He gave it his best shot, and yet still I rise, never to give in. I have God on the inside of me. The enemy can't touch God and he is limited in what he can do to me.

The good news is living a righteous life has its rewards. **John 3:21 AMP says, "But he who practices truth [who does what is right]** comes out into the Light; so that his works may be plainly shown to be what they are-wrought with God [divinely prompted, done with God's help, in dependence upon Him]." I purpose in my heart to do good. I don't live a life one way before others and another way behind closed doors. What you see is what you get. Maybe what you will see is the same me, but with a tad bit more layers of clothing on.

Jesus faced many distractions, but He never gave into one of them. Through all of the noise He managed to keep His eyes fixed on doing the will of God. **Hebrews 4:15 NIV says, "For we do not have a high priest who is unable to empathize with our weaknesses, but we have one who has been tempted in every way, just as we are, yet he did not sin."** Temptation is a distraction. When temptations came, knowing full well they were mere distractions, Jesus spoke to each temptation declaring the word of God.

Jesus was confronted with distractions back to back. In **Matthew 4:1-11 MSG**, it talks about the first test where Jesus was fasting forty days and forty nights. The Devil said, **"Since you are God's Son, speak the word that will turn these stones into loaves of bread." Jesus countered, "It takes more than bread to stay alive. It takes a steady stream of words from God's mouth."** When you know your God, you will not allow others to pull you away from Him. Man does not live by bread alone, but by every word that proceeds out of the mouth of God. Our dependency is on Him.

The next test where Jesus was taken to the Holy City, the devil sat Him on the top of the Temple and said, **"Since you are God's Son, jump." Jesus countered, "Don't you dare test the Lord your God."** There is nothing the Lord won't do for us. However, the fact that He gave us His son Jesus lets us know He has already proven His love and demonstrated it toward us. We don't have to prove to others through tests that God can do a thing. Faith teaches us to believe that God can do all things. The knowledge of all that God has already done is sufficient to shut the mouth of any devil.

The third test, the devil took him to the peak of a huge mountain. He pointed out all the earth's kingdoms, how glorious they all were. **Then he said, "They're yours, lock, stock and barrel. Just go down on your knees and worship me, and they're yours." Jesus' refusal was curt: "Beat it, Satan! Worship the Lord your God,**

and only him. Serve him with absolute single-heartedness." Don't waste time playing around with the enemy. Speak to the distractions and you will see them and they will leave you. Far too long we served the devil. When we entered into the saving Grace of Jesus, we were secure once and for all. The devil has lost again.

Your test will come back to back just as Jesus' did. God doesn't want you to shy away from the test. Nor does He want you to respond out of panic. The Word worked for Jesus first of all because Jesus is the Word. Secondly, the Word worked because it is the truth that cancels out wrong and evil. Manipulation cannot stand in the face of God's Word. The Word rises to every occasion.

You have to stand in your full authority when the test comes. Get the Word in you, so that it can began discrediting the enemy and silencing his lies. Do not allow anyone or anything to cause you to shrink back with what you know about or believe about God.

I rely and depend on God wholeheartedly, test or not. I know God is with me, but I am aware of the tactics of the enemy and alert to the evil the devil conspires. Sometimes we can see clearly the schemes the enemy has devised for us. But there are times when we are blindsided. The scripture says in **John 10:10 NIV, "The thief comes only to steal and kill and destroy. I have come that they may have life, and have it to the full."** While the enemy has a plan of destruction; God has a plan to prosper you. Those tactics and schemes of the enemy can't stand up to God.

Don't allow the plans of the enemy to override your thinking. Guard your thinking. If he can bring confusion in your life, causing your thinking to be warped, he is happy. Of course, God is all powerful and can wipe out the enemy without moving from His throne. But every time you have victory over the enemy, refusing to compromise your peace, God is happy. Truth be told, the enemy is not after you. He comes after what matters most to God, which happens to be you. Knowing full well the enemy is no match for God; he comes at you in an attempt to get to God. If at all possible, his desire is to cause you to abort the real plan God has for you.

The plan God has for you is the same plan, whether you are going through trials or not. The hope you operate under comes through as the sun peeping through the clouds or shining through your window.

You have hope because you believe God is the true and living God. The more you make your hope known, the more He confirms what you hope for. Though you believe before you know, when God lets you in on portions of His plan, you believe more and you know without doubt.

You can best believe His plan does not resemble the adversary's plan. The best advice I can give you is to carry out the portion God brings to your attention while you await further instructions. God will give you the next set of instructions once you complete the first set satisfactorily.

Meanwhile, if you depend on the Lord, you won't have to worry about your plans. Whatever you do, if you commit to the Lord, your plans will be established. **Proverbs 16:3 NLT says, "Commit your actions to the Lord, and your plans will succeed."** When you cooperate with the plan instead of fighting it, you reap the benefits of a productive and healthy life.

Don't allow the distractions of life to hinder you in the things of God. It's easy to get off track or off course when you focus on the distraction, opposed to where you're headed. Experienced drivers don't allow pot holes or detours to keep them from their destination. They go around the potholes, take the detour and land at their destination.

In the beginning of my driving history, I drove straight through pot holes. I didn't know how to avoid them. Sometimes, they appeared out of nowhere, leaving me with little time to go around them. One pothole was so large when I hit it, it felt like the entire bottom of the car was snatched off. The more I drove, the faster I learned how to avoid the potholes.

When I lived in DC, not only was I a new driver, but I was just learning to drive a stick shift. I was not familiar with driving on the streets of D.C. and I only knew one way to get home when I went out. One particular day, as I was returning home, I noticed a road block. The police detoured traffic in another direction, which meant I could not go home as usual. I panicked. As I approached the officer, he motioned for me to take the detour. I began screaming, crying and hitting the steering wheel and yelling, "I don't know where to go!" The officer could have responded in many ways, but instead he favored me. He moved the orange barriers and granted me access.

God sure favored me that day. Who knows how long I would have been riding around in circles lost. Favor caused me to keep on driving after that day instead of giving in to fear. It also provoked me to find other routes to get home. Today, I drive everywhere I want to go regardless to whether I am familiar with the route or not. I still manage to get lost, but I don't worry about it because I have tapped into God's divine favor. He gave me wisdom as well as tools, such as navigation, OnStar, maps, or MapQuest to get me through.

As heirs of Jesus, we are led by the Spirit of God as sons. **Romans 8:14-15 ESV says, "For you did not receive the spirit of slavery to fall back into fear, but you have received the Spirit of adoption as sons, by whom we cry, "Abba! Father!"** Because you are led by the Holy Spirit, you no longer have a spirit of fear. You can bypass every hindrance and distraction. For the purpose of this example, the distraction serves as the pothole, and the detour works as the hindrance. Just as I overcame running into potholes and the fear of forced detours, I can just as easily overcome the distractions and hindrances.

Distractions can show up in many forms, but God has already equipped you to escape the diversion. You do not have to give your full attention to anything but God. Nor do you have to divide your attention between anything else and God. It's a choice in what you concentrate on. **Philippians 4:8 KJV, "Finally, brethren, whatsoever things are true, whatsoever things are honest, whatsoever things are just, whatsoever things are pure, whatsoever things are lovely, whatsoever things are of good report, if there be any virtue, and if there be any praise, think on these things."** When you're thinking on all these things, distractions don't stand a chance. Focus more of your time on what is going right, opposed to the negative and what didn't go right.

The Hope of Glory . . .

> ➢ *Colossians 1:27 NLT, "For God wanted them to know that the riches and glory of Christ are for you Gentiles,*

too. And this is the secret: Christ lives in you. This gives you assurance of sharing his glory."

The writer penned what my heart expresses, "My hope is built on nothing less than Jesus' blood and righteousness. I dare not trust the sweetest frame but wholly lean on Jesus' name. On Christ the solid rock I stand, all other ground is sinking sand." The hope of Glory lives in you. Yet He surrounds your physical atmosphere as well as your inner being.

If you are not careful, you will work harder for the things of the world than for the treasures of the kingdom. The invested labor and continuous struggle you make in sharing the gospel of Jesus is far more rewarding than investing labor and struggling, but never receiving any measure of goodness, faithfulness or righteousness.

The language that comes out of your mouth is an indication of what you believe and how you think. Your actions are what you are judged by. If you say you love God but refused to follow His way, then you don't really love Him. You must trust Him, which pushes Him to act on your behalf. When He responds, He brings on board justice and highlights your righteousness as an added bonus.

David says in **Psalm 37:5-6 ESV, "Commit your way to the LORD; trust in him, and he will act. He will bring forth your righteousness as the light, and your justice as the noonday."** God is committed to you. He doesn't ask you to do anything that He has not done or is not aware of. At the same time, it's a relationship that requires action. Your action causes Him to take action. If you're fighting tooth and nail, determined to commit your way to what is pleasing to you, you will not experience or receive the plethora of blessings with your name stamped on them.

Why go through life resisting and struggling, trying to change the plan for your life. You lose out every time you try to take matters into your own hands. Just surrender and reap the rewards! What you're looking for and searching for in the world will never satisfy you. It will never be enough. Once you acquire all you think you want, the newness of it all will begin to fade. You will always desire more and seek to gain more.

I know when I lay down to sleep at night; it is not the stuff I have acquired that causes me to rest. It's not the material things that bring me complete joy. It is not the accomplishments that fulfill me. It's not the work I am doing that grants me peace. It is the love that exudes from my Heavenly Father. It's the assurance on the inside of me that encompasses my inner place by the Holy Spirit. It's the warm blood running through my body screaming redeemed by my Jesus, the Christ. The hope that I have in God the Father, God the Son and God the Holy Spirit continually renews my strength.

The connection I have is the only real connection I need. It's funny how sometimes, when I drive through the tolls on the highway, the person in the booth often asks how we are doing. Sometimes I smile. Though no one is physically in the car with me, God, Jesus and Holy Spirit really are physically in the car with me. The person in the toll booth clearly sees more than just me. We are surrounded daily with goodness, and love.

I do not resist God or His presence. I do not reject Jesus or His presence. I do not hide the Holy Spirit or His presence. They are a package deal that I accept wholeheartedly. My three in one love package is what I live for and by.

John explains well in **Chapter 15 verses 1-4 ESV** the role Jesus and God plays. He says, **"I am the vine, and my Father is the vinedresser. Every branch in me that does not bear fruit he takes away, and every branch that does bear fruit he prunes, that it may bear more fruit. Already you are clean because of the word that I have spoken to you. Abide in me, and I in you. As the branch cannot bear fruit by itself, unless it abides in the vine, neither can you, unless you abide in me."** That says to me that you cannot bypass Jesus or God. It is like running into a brick wall that will not crumble or fall. If you attempt to go another route in hopes of avoiding God, you will find counterfeit. If you attempt to go another route in hopes of escaping Jesus, you will not be granted access.

On the other hand, Jesus is laying out the chain of command so that you can get it right from the start. Just like on your job, in your church or place of business, protocol has to be respected and followed. It's like love and marriage, you can't have one without the other. We are in this relationship wrought with love that is secured, obedience that was demonstrated and abiding power that will comfort, while sustaining us.

Without God, it would be as a maze. You cannot exclude God and expect to reach your destiny in one piece. People without God are wandering through, circling back and are being trapped in places they can't figure out how to get out of. It's almost like being discombobulated. The fact of the matter is, God cannot be erased from the map. Even if an individual has decided he or she can maneuver through life without God, He is still present.

When you think about children, especially if you have them, though some children may stop talking to their parents it doesn't change the fact that God ordained them as parents of the children. You can ignore your natural father, but he is still your father. The same is so with God, you can certainly try to run from God, but unlike your earthly father, there is no place you can run where He won't know where you are. Just because He doesn't say anything to you, doesn't mean He cannot see you. Sometimes God asks questions that He already knows the answer to. He provokes you to think and causes you to see for yourself what's really in your heart.

The good news about abiding in God is He doesn't just throw you out into the world unarmed. He gives you information on a need to know basis, and on as much as you can handle basis. Outside of that, God already provided a manual for you, the Bible, (Biblical Instruction before Leaving Earth). He already gave you preachers on every corner. Most importantly, He gave His Son Jesus Christ, the Messiah, the great Savior and demonstrator. He gave Holy Spirit, the Mighty Comforter and Teacher, and He gives Himself, El Shaddai, The Almighty All-Sufficient God who protects and provides.

When you connect with God, your power source, you receive power to live out the plan. Before any assignment is ever given to you, God encircles you with strength and makes your pathway straight. He doesn't set you up for failure. David said in **Psalm 18:32 NIV, "It is God who arms me with strength and keeps my way secure."** In God there is certainty, and there is security. When you are doing what you are supposed to be doing, God will continue to renew your strength. When things get rough, He will make sure you come out on top. He's an All-Encompassing God. Everything you need, God has.

Wisdom lets us know there are right and wrong ways to do anything. And because there are options, we have choices. While the choice is yours to make, God continues to surround you with His goodness. The scripture says in **Proverbs 12:15 NIV, "The way of fools seems right to them, but the wise listen to advice.** You really don't know what you are doing outside of God. But God knows what He is doing outside of you. In your ignorance, as we all have been ignorant at some point; don't be so determined to do things your way. Fools value their own wisdom.

Proverbs 15:22 NIV says, "Plans fail for lack of counsel, but with many advisers they succeed." Refusing good advice only results in watching your plans fail. When someone offers a solution to your problem, or guidance in a dilemma, and you don't take it, you are a fool. I didn't say it, but I interpreted it through Proverbs 12:15. We don't always consult people, but it's apparent when we don't consult God.

David says in **Psalm 32:8-11 ESV, "I will instruct you and teach you in the way you should go; I will counsel you with my eye upon you. Be not like a horse or a mule, without understanding, which must be curbed with bit and bridle, or it will or it will not stay near you. Many are the sorrows of the wicked, but steadfast love surrounds the one who trusts in the LORD. Be glad in the LORD, and rejoice, O righteous, and shout for joy, all you upright in heart!"** David was talking about following sound instruction for staying on the righteous path. He was encouraging the people to be God-affirmers, not God-defiers. David was showing us how to stay on track with God.

Certainly stick with the plan, but don't just follow the plan, enjoy it, rejoice over it. It really is a good plan! If you will put one hundred percent toward pursuing the plan God has for you, it most definitely will be accomplished. What that one hundred percent looks like is you surrendering your will wholeheartedly to God.

You have heard it said, "The steps of a good man are ordered by the Lord." **Psalm 37:23 NIV says, "The Lord makes firm the steps of the one who delights in him; though he may stumble, he will not fall, for the LORD upholds him with his hand."** Try to escape the plan, or reject the plan and see how far you get in life with the plan you come up with. If you are not taking delight in God and the things of God, you will fall flat on your face every time. You will hit rock bottom so fast, you'll be sitting there trying to figure out how you got there.

It's easier for me to do right than to do wrong. Both require making a choice. One has consequences and the other has rewards. For me doing wrong takes more effort and comes with more problems. The issue I have with wrong is you cannot tell it what it can or cannot bring along the ride. You go from doing wrong to dealing with feelings for doing wrong. Then there are those consequences you anticipated and those you didn't calculate. Wrong attaches whatever it wants to and there is little you can do about it. It's a trap. Once you get lured into wrong, either you continue doing wrong and accept everything it offers, or you cut your losses and flee.

Doing wrong proves costly. You only end up with more problems. **James 4:17 ESV** says, **"So whoever knows the right thing to do and fails to do it, for him it is sin."** So not only are there consequences for doing the wrong thing, but there is penalty too. **Romans 6:23 NIV** says, **"The wages of sin is death, but the gift of God is eternal life in Christ Jesus our Lord."** I don't know about you, but I prefer to receive the gift of God than the wages of sin. Every time I do right, I know I glorify and honor God.

Before you connect to any man or woman, first connect to God. So many people face Church hurt, abuse, you name it, but a lot of that can be avoided if you only seek God before taking a step. Every church I joined I sought the Lord first. I visited until I heard a resounding yes. I got clearance each time. There were some churches where I heard nothing, so I did nothing. At the same time, when I was released from any church it was evident that my season was up. I left decently and in order.

I would not be living above insanity without God's direction. I certainly wouldn't be on the clear path I am on without God ordering my steps. When I look back over my life, I am extremely grateful for my heavenly Father. I credit Him for bringing me into the new life full of truth, grace, mercy and authority.

The psalmist Mahalia Jackson sang, "How I got over." She said her soul look back and wonders how she made it over. There's a difference between getting over because of some scheme you came up with, and getting OVER through the Grace of God. We're not talking about trying to manipulate the plan, but allowing the Grace of God to carry you over. Mahalia was rejoicing because she knew she had followed the plan and God brought her over many barriers, and hurdles and ultimately salvation.

Just as with Mahalia Jackson, God offers us a reassuring presence. Nothing we do escapes Him. Nothing we say gets passed Him. We are an open book to Him. David said in **Psalm 139:1-4 NLT, "O LORD, you have examined my heart and know everything about me. You know when I sit down or stand up. You know my thoughts even when I'm far away. You see me when I travel and when I rest at home. You know everything I do. You know what I am going to say even before I say it, LORD."** This information alone should cause you to surrender to God willingly. Many work overtime trying to fool people, and though they manage to pull the wool over the eyes of some, God knows the real deal.

The Travel Itinerary . . .

> ➤ *Proverbs 3:23 MSG, "You'll travel safely; you'll neither tire nor trip."*

Everyone comes to earth under a plan created by God. Everything you do (every assignment you carry out) has relevance. I reiterate everything is connected, even the assignment of writing. My obedience to write is a part of my call. The written word that's inspired through me by God was a part of His plan to reach the multitude. As a result of my assignment to write, I am able to offer practical truths unleashing hope through encouragement. My writing focuses on life's experiences and wisdom.

The fact that you are reading this today means I am on target in this phase of my journey. Because I am on target, you get your treasures that are in me. The gift God has given me isn't just for me; it's for me to generously and compassionately disburse to you and others. Everything I learn, I pass on. Earth is a learning ground, and if you must cohabitate on earth, you might as well use the lessons to your advantage. My advantage is to give you every advantage, providing tools for your journey. After all, the most important thing in life is People. People! That's what it's all about.

Sometimes we feel we can't live with people. The truth of the matter is we cannot afford to live without people. God chose to create us and He chose to live with us. In fact, He chose to live in us. We're His most prized possession. We're what make the journey on earth worthwhile. Jesus came to earth because we were on earth. Had not we been here, He would not have needed to come. God's love caused Him to want to rescue us from the lures on earth. Not that earth is a bad place, but the enemy has polluted it with evil, through vices.

In order for you to get what God have given me for you; I have to consistently be obedient. In my obedience to God, Graduate School was on the radar yet again. My husband joked with me saying, "Don't get another degree that doesn't pay you." Though I got the punch line, the degrees I have pay me when you get your healing, breakthrough, and deliverance. When you receive inspiration, motivation, encouragement through something I've experienced, done or said, I get paid. I get paid every time God uses me. It's all a part of the plan for my life, and that benefits you.

Dr. Myles Monroe said, "The greatest tragedy in life is not death, but a life without a purpose." Everyone has purpose. God created each of us with a plan in mind, and purpose that matters to Him. With that being said, of course He wants you to live your life on purpose. That purpose should entail obedience to God. I just believe the more obedient you are, the clearer your purpose will become.

So, what is the plan for your life? Follow the will of God and you will see it unfold before your very eyes. God's will is good, pleasing and perfect. Paul says in **Romans 12:2 ESV, "Do not be conformed to this world, but be transformed by the renewal of your mind, that by testing you may discern what is the will of God, what is good and acceptable and perfect."** Your purpose begins with you thinking differently and positively.

In other words the whole chapter of Romans One sums up what you ought to be doing to satisfy the will of God. You must become a living sacrifice. That means you consecrate and offer yourself to God. You can do that because of the gift of Grace God has so generously bestowed upon you. Determine to live for God.

Paul highlights the marks of the true Christian which ultimately reveals you have to love God, and do what He says. When you love God you keep His commandments. When you do what He says, you operate under the plan He created for you.

The purpose God had in mind for you in the beginning was never void of Him. Though He knows who will reject Him and who will accept Him, everyone is given the same opportunity. We either accept truth (God) or we live with the lie (the enemy). I choose truth.

The truth is, in order to not be conformed to this world; you must overcome the things in the world. The world consists of the lust of the flesh, the lust of the eyes, and the pride of life. **1 John 2:15-16 ESV** says, **"Do not love the world or the things in the world. If anyone loves the world, the love of the Father is not in him. For all that is in the world, the desires of the flesh and the desires of the eyes and pride of life is not from the Father but is from the world."** Jesus has already overcome the world, but He did not take you out of the world.

While you are in the world, God wants you to give your total self over to Him. When you yield your will to God submitting yourself to Him, you offer yourself as a living sacrifice. As a living sacrifice, God's will is able to be done in your life. Righteousness and Obedience is God's will for all of His children. You must continually offer yourself in service to God. It's an expectation to live acceptable unto God.

What's your earthly reward in all of this righteous living and righteous doing? **Isaiah 32:17 NIV says, "The fruit of that righteousness will be peace; the effect will be quietness and confidence forever."** That sounds good enough to me. I have been on both sides of the fence, with no peace and with peace. I choose peace any day. When I please God I feel better about myself and I am at peace. The end result of peace equates to me as heaven. The essence of quietness equates to heaven.

The fact that I am with God now gives me great confidence. I know when it's all said and done and I am with God later, I will have that same confidence. I have walked without confidence; it sure feels good to have it. I think I will hold on to it.

When I began pastoring, I heard reports from members of different churches regarding their issues, church hurt and problems they faced. I thanked God daily for the peace we experienced in serving Him at our church. I wanted to tell those people to come join me, but I would rather be small and at peace, than large and chaotic. Though I don't run from growth, I treasure peace. So instead, I advised them, if God told you to go to a particular church, then submit until He releases you, and above all, get the lesson.

I sure would have loved to have shepherded those people with the love and compassion of God, but once a person says God told them to join a church, that's typically home for them. I believe if you were positioned by God, His grace is sufficient for you even when the storms rage. If you were not positioned by God, but you went on your own accord, (as many of them did), then leave on your own accord, or stay there and grin and bear it. You should not leave a church because you cannot have your way. However, I can give you reasons when you should leave.

People don't always join churches under the unction of the Holy Spirit. Most determining factors are a result of the choir, status of the preacher or how many members they have. Before I was ordained as Pastor, I made sure the Holy Spirit gave me the okay to join any church. Once I heard Him say it was safe, I confirmed He was telling me to join. He hasn't led me astray. I didn't choose what I wanted; I chose what the Holy Spirit told me to choose.

My mother and father chose my first church, St. Matthew's Lutheran Church. My mother allowed me to join the choir of the neighborhood church, Forest Baptist Church, though I wasn't a member. When I left home, I accepted Jesus as Lord and Savior and joined New Hope Freewill Baptist Church. I didn't stay long, but I got what I needed. From there I joined Fort Foote Baptist Church under the unction of the Holy Spirit. After leaving the area, I joined Mt. Gilead Full Gospel International Ministries which was by recommendation of my previous pastor, but ultimately under the unction of the Holy Spirit.

Though no church is perfect, I did pretty well following the leading of the Holy Spirit to add to my overall growth. I don't church hop. If the pastor has integrity, teaches the word and I am able to apply that word, I hang in there. I am blessed to have had two trustworthy pastors, Rev. Dr. Joseph Lyles and Bishop Daniel Robertson, Jr.

If you have a call to Pastor, what you want in a pastor is also what you should be as a pastor. I care about people, but I look for integrity, character and honesty. I am genuine and I strive to do unto others as I would have them do unto me. I am compassionate but not soft. I am stern but not judgmental. I believe in people, but I trust God. I go above and beyond the call of duty when it comes to the things of God, and I don't understand when others don't have that same commitment or passion.

Those two pastors exhibited commitment and passion. They helped me to move from a babe in Christ to a mature leader. I went from getting saved to leading others to Christ. It wasn't long before I was able to demonstrate the word by showing others how to live out the Word of God. I discovered early on that discipleship is most important. If you first learn how to become a disciple, you will do great at making disciples of others.

The Path . . .

> ➤ *Proverbs 4:26 ESV, "Ponder the path for your feet; then all your ways will be sure."*

The plan for your expected end begins with salvation. God wants you to have a future and hope. He wants you have a posterity (future generations of descendants/people). Life with the Father does not end. However, life with the Father cannot begin unless you allow Jesus to be Savior.

We know Jesus as the Great High Priest; He was appointed and exalted by God. This leads me to a sidebar, **Hebrews 5:4 AMP** says, **"One does not appropriate for himself the honor of being high priest, but he is called by God and receives it of Him."** Too many people are exalting themselves. One vehicle being used is the internet. Jesus was designated and recognized and saluted by God as High Priest, which says to me, as it concerns your call, make sure God recognizes it. It would be a shame to tell the world you are called to do something that God didn't ordain or put His stamp of approval on.

God ordained Jesus. **Hebrews 5:9 AMP** says, **"He became the Author and Source of eternal salvation to all those who give heed and obey him."** Man may have witnessed His strong suits, gifts and talents but it was God who affirmed His call for leading others to Him. Just as man may witness your call, it is God who places the call within you before man ever sees it.

Jesus lived out His purpose of saving others from the guilt, ruin, shame, and bondage sin caused. He operated in His call long after He departed earth. He appeared to Saul on the road to Damascus. Saul was converted through the voice of Jesus **(Acts 9)**. Jesus paved the way for salvation and continues to make the way possible for all who are receptive. His call was so impactful that it still manifests action today.

Jesus says in **John 6:51 KJV, "I am the living bread which came down from heaven; if any man eat of this bread, he shall live forever: and the bread that I will give is my flesh, which I will give for the life of the world."** Jesus is the beginning and Jesus is the end. One thing is for sure, you cannot say He is not consistent. You have to acknowledge Him in the beginning, and you must go through Him in the end.

The scripture says in **John 6:53 ESV, "So Jesus said to them, "Truly, truly, I say to you, unless you eat the flesh of the Son of Man and drink his blood, you have no life in you."** Without Jesus, there is no real life in you on earth and certainly no real life in you after you leave this earth. The plan was for you to come to Jesus, believe in Jesus, and abide in Jesus. Only then can you know the Father. We were created to fellowship and commune with the Father.

The plan is all-inclusive. **1 John 5:11-13 GNT says, "This testimony is this: God has given us eternal life, and this life has its source in his Son. Whoever has the Son has this life; whoever does not have the Son of God does not have life."** Whoever rejects the Son rejects life. Many don't believe this testimony, but I certainly do. I want the life, and I wholeheartedly, unashamedly accept the life. This acceptance involves abiding.

The reality is this: If you believe in Jesus, you will know beyond the shadow of a doubt that you have eternal life. Believing in Jesus gives you the boldness and freedom to go into God's presence and freely ask for what you need according to His will. You can be confident that He is listening, and expect to receive what you ask for.

Though I am not a needy person, I ask for a lot from God. Much of what I ask for, I believe I deserve. Some things I simply want. I get much of what I ask for. Some things I don't ask for because I know I will get it. One example would be when I applied for a position that had promotion potential. I told God I was not going to plead for Him to give me the position because I knew He would. I prayed, "But if it is your will for me to have this position, I will take it." The position was filled, and I didn't get it. Later I discovered things about the office that made me praise God I didn't get the position. I never want to jump out of the frying pan into the fire, so to speak.

Sometimes we beg and plead for things knowing full well they aren't the best thing for us. We kick and scream having temper tantrums when God says no, but what we don't know is why He said no. God knows what goes on behind the scenes in a place, and He knows those associated with that place inside out. Maybe He is sparing you from what you are begging for. Or maybe He just wants better for you.

One day as I sat at my work station, at approximately 2:30 p.m., I began feeling nauseous. I wanted to get up immediately and go home. I suddenly felt the desire to be home. I had leave, but I did not want to use it. I looked out the window and uttered, "Lord I want to go home! I want to go home now! I can't do this today!"

I sat there in silence looking out of the window when all of a sudden I heard a loud boom. The power throughout the entire building went out. There was no access to the computers or the telephones, and the lights were out. I raised my eyebrow and sat there quietly; shortly after I proceeded to pack my things. No later than 3:30 p.m., the office closed due to the outage. I ran out the door in full speed as the character "Madea" from the Tyler Perry movie did when she was released from jail.

I am confident that God is listening to me, and I expect what I ask for. However, I do not ask amiss. **James 4:3 KJV, "Ye ask, and receive not, because ye ask amiss, that ye may consume it upon your lusts."** You cannot ask for things that only bring you pleasure. You won't get it if you ask with wrong motives.

God knew I wasn't just being slothful. He knew the difference between me wanting to leave because of how I felt, opposed to wanting to leave to avoid having to work. Getting God involved was a blessing in that; I didn't have to use my earned leave. The plan has many benefits when you follow it. That's just one example on a smaller scale of the things God does for me.

To sum it up, the plan was initiated when God sent us to earth. Just like Jesus came through the birth canal of a woman, you did too. When God sends us to earth, we come as babes, kicking and screaming trying to find our way. We go through the toddler stage, reach puberty, and then we go on to become adults, still kicking and screaming trying to find our way. And it was God's intention for all of us to make it, but unfortunately some of us don't make it. Sadly, some of us struggle and wrestle more than we ever should.

When Jesus came to earth, it wasn't a bed of roses for Him either, but He survived it. It's as if He said, "Look, I'm going to come down and show you how to do this, but you have to follow me and do it the way I'm showing you." Some of us get it quicker than others. Some of us catch on faster. This whole life, the entire plan that God created was always for us to win. It was always for us to catch on to and follow.

The Learning Curve . . .

> *I Timothy 2:1-6 ESV, "First of all, then, I urge that supplications, prayers, intercessions, and thanksgivings be made for all people, for kings and all who are in high positions, that we may lead a peaceful and quiet life, godly and dignified in every way. This is good, and it is pleasing in the sight of God our Savior, who desires all people to be saved and to come to the knowledge of the truth. For there is one God, and there is one mediator between God and men, the man Christ Jesus, who gave himself as a ransom for all, which is the testimony given at the proper time."*

Learn all you can while you can. Too many allow opportunities to pass them by. Whatever setting I am in, I look to see if there is something that I can take away from being there. When you are an observer as I am, you see things that haven't even crossed the mind of others. It can be something as simple as seeing someone discipline there child in a milder manner than you used to. That observation could soon become something you choose to model. It could be that you visited someone's house and was exposed to their organizational pattern, and choose to model that. Whatever it is, we are ever learning.

Bishop Robertson often says, "Some things are taught and some things are caught." Jesus taught so much. And just hanging around Him and hearing about what He did and looking at the things He did, you can catch so much. Catch Life, that's what it is really all about, Life. My prayer is that you open your heart to the life God has for you and enjoy it. God really does know what He is doing.

The plan is consistent, but it comes with a route that you must take. Of course, there will be detours along the way from time to time. They prevent you from going too fast. Sometimes it's to avoid familiarity. We tend to get comfortable with doing things, and they become habit forming. Just as we get too familiar with things, we become too familiar with people. The reverence and the respect fade away.

The connections, God, Jesus, and Holy Spirit who are literally stationed at every turn in life are most essential in getting us through life's journey. Because people are involved in our journeys, however long our journey may be, you can count on sideshow distractions. Before you attack the person, remember the enemy is the distraction behind the show. If he can get you to focus on the person, you won't focus on him. In shifting the focus, he has free reign to run amok.

Nevertheless, we have the full assurance that the Hope of Glory has gone before us preparing our way. Because God the Father, the Son and the Holy Spirit has made their abode with us, we have confidence. God makes provision for His children. Jesus provokes access of the provision from the Father for the children. The Holy Spirit enables us to live out the provision the Father has given, provoked by Jesus.

If this were a travel agency, Jesus makes the travel arrangements for us. God lays out the travel itinerary for us. And the Holy Spirit accompanies us on the trip. Every path we take He is there. We have the best agent ever. The only time we don't travel first class is when we take it upon ourselves to make our own reservations.

When God created the plan, as He so eloquently laid out for us; He knew exactly what He was doing. Get to really know God and I guarantee, you will soon stop asking what your purpose is and what the plan is for your life. Do the first thing He tells you to do, and He will give you a second thing to do. It will become repetitive, one thing after the other. You can expect Him to give you something to do just like clockwork. Focus on getting those things done, and before you know it, you will be so busy you will replace the question of what you're supposed to be doing.

I can assure you of three things. The plan will always be bigger than just you. It will always involve people. You will never be without something to do or someone to help.

The Heart of God . . .

> *I John 3:1-3 ESV, "See what kind of love the Father has given to us that we should be called children of God; and so we are. The reason why the world does not know us is that it did not know him. Beloved, we are God's children now, and what we will be has not yet appeared; but we know that when he appears we shall be like him, because we shall see him as he is. ³ And everyone who thus hopes in him purifies himself as he is pure."*

We are to immolate God. How great is the love the Father has lavished on us that we should be called children of God. Because we are His children, we want to be like Him. If we are like Him, we want to do what He does. In doing what He does, we have to abide by His rules.

You will always be required to love, forgive, and help others. You will always have divine help. Your life will exemplify God. Your prayers will exemplify Jesus. Your heart will exemplify Holy Spirit.

You will have hope, joy, and love. You will pursue peace and wisdom. You will bestow grace and mercy unto others. You will exhibit perseverance, and become longsuffering. You will prosper and be in good health.

You will edify the body. You will be God's glory carrier impacting lives upon lives. You will be as surefooted as a deer, able to tread upon the heights. You will surrender your will until it becomes His will. What you won't have to do is wonder or ponder what your purpose is, or why you were sent to earth.

Hebrews 3:7-13 NIV says, **"So, as the Holy Spirit says: "Today, if you hear his voice, do not harden your hearts as you did in the rebellion, during the time of testing in the wilderness, where your ancestors tested and tried me, though for forty years they saw what I did. That is why I was angry with that generation; I said, 'Their hearts are always going astray, and they have not known my ways.' So I declared an oath in my anger, 'They shall never enter my rest.'**

See to it, brothers and sisters, that none of you has a sinful, unbelieving heart that turns away from the living God. But encourage one another daily, as long as it is called "Today," so that none of you may be hardened by sin's deceitfulness." It's a warning indeed to keep us from repeating history. But we have to listen and obey.

Hebrews 3:16-19 NIV further asks, **"Who were they who heard and rebelled? Were they not all those Moses led out of Egypt? And with whom was he angry for forty years? Was it not with those who sinned, whose bodies perished in the wilderness? And to whom did God swear that they would never enter his rest if not to those who disobeyed? So we see that they were not able to enter, because of their unbelief.** You certainly won't follow the plan of God if you don't believe in God. If you are disobedient to God, and have no fear of going astray, you most definitely will not be accustomed to His ways. Neither will you enter into His rest. I want to be so close to God that I hear His heartbeat. Wherever He is, that's where I desire to be.

Being in the secret place with God is being close to His heart. To know that I have a place in God's heart means the world to me. David was after God's heart. If you are going to go after anyone's heart, it definitely should be God's. Too often people want to win the heart of man. I have been there and done that myself. And though I may have succeeded, it is not lasting nor is it as fulfilling as having your name, your cares, and your destiny on God's heart.

David said in **Psalm 27:4-5 ESV, "One thing have I asked of the Lord, that will I seek after: that I may dwell in the house of the Lord all the days of my life, to gaze upon the beauty of the Lord and to inquire in his temple. For he will hide me in his shelter in the day of trouble; he will conceal me under the cover of his tent; he will lift me high upon a rock."** God has certainly hid me in His shelter in the day of trouble. He has kept trouble at bay in many instances. There have been times where He concealed me and I knew He was at work. Also there were times where He lifted me high above things that I wasn't aware of what was going on. I don't have access to all the details and I don't need to, but I am grateful for His shelter.

God has you on His radar. He will see to it that you have exactly what you need in your time of distress. He delivers in all situations, be it through scripture, a song, a dream, vision, or through someone else. He doesn't stop at anything when it relates to getting to you the necessities of life.

My Response to the Plan . . .

> ➢ *Galatians 2:20 NIV, "I have been crucified with Christ and I no longer live, but Christ lives in me. The life I now live in the body, I live by faith in the Son of God, who loved me and gave himself for me."*

The Sovereign Lord is my strength. In Him will I forever put my trust. I trust every aspect of the plan, line upon line, precept upon precept. I will serve Him graciously all the days of my life. I vow to share the good news, which is the gospel of Jesus. I vow to share the love of God which was demonstrated in the life, death, burial and resurrection of Jesus Christ, the Messiah.

The plan caused me to venture from the innocent little scrawny country girl from the south into the person I am today. Growing up with humble beginnings, knowing deep within my heart that there had to be more to life than what I was experiencing, I searched for more. Filled with southern dialect, I embraced city life. I was naive to the customs of manipulation, but wide eyed with high hopes for good. My heart was as open as the Atlantic Ocean.

Coming from a place with a good heart and a genuine spirit, I was shielded some, but still managed to be thrust in daring, tempting and luring situations. Some of life's traps I fell into. Others I escaped. My morals never granted me access to be devoured. I never got in over my head. For the most part, I attempted to play it safe.

I experienced what many went though, trial and error. I wasn't one to live on the edge, I never pushed the envelope going too far, though I participated in things I knew I should not have. Somehow, despite what I did, I had enough sense to whisper to God for help, pray to Him when in need and yell Help when I found myself in desperate situations. I think I was one of the blessed ones early on. God had His hands on me from a child.

I am not going to fabricate a life racked with sin because it wasn't the case. I had morals even back then. I got caught up in sin, but mostly tried to do the right thing. To show you the kind of life I lived, when I wrote my first book and disclosed some of the things I did, my family accused me of lying. I wish I were.

I have lost much, but I have gained greater in return. Regardless to what I experienced, I was determined to not allow those situations to alter my personality. I was never a magnet for trouble, nor did I go looking for it. When trouble found me, I didn't lie down and die with it.

Though there were hiccups along the way in my life, I was known as morally and ethically sound. I pretty much stayed to myself, yet I did what most teenagers and unsaved adults do. I sinned. I had a long list of things I said I would never do. Some of the things that I prided myself on because I hadn't done, I eventually did. But I was a fast learner. It didn't take me long to figure out when a wrong really wasn't right.

Over my life span, I have seen much from the low end of sin to the high end. I have never been too judgmental because I have learned if you are quick to judge others, sooner or later the very thing you judged has the potential of finding its way to you or your family. I believed then and now in giving others the benefit of the doubt. As a trustworthy person, I believed heavily in loyalty. Because I was loyal, I expected that same loyalty from others.

I came from a small town; however, it wasn't void of sin. Small town folk sometimes do just as much if not more as people from larger cities. Crime occurs in every neighborhood, and sin happens in every individual. You may not practice or habitually sin, but all have sinned and come short of the glory of God.

Looking back, I believed in some people more than I should have. As a result, I trusted more than I needed to. Open trust can come at a cost. When you put your trust in others, it is easy to be taken for granted, used and even abused. My trusting in some of those people left me with bruises, scars, hurt and pain. Fortunately, the learning experiences I received after extending trust and being wounded ultimately gave me strength, wisdom, tenacity and resilience.

Through all of the hardship, as well as good times, I am most proud that I never lost my way in the things of God. I started out believing He was God and regardless to my disobedience I always knew He was God. I didn't view my disobedience as rejecting God as the creator or Jesus as Savior. My issue was, as is with many, I didn't want to stop doing the foolish things I did.

I endured enough heartache that pushed me into relationship with God by my early twenties. I think I always wanted to do what was right, but influences persuaded me to go in the wrong direction. Excuses can prevent us from doing what we know we should.

My life took a turn for the good spiritually not long after my husband and I had our daughter. I determined to run hard after God. I had so many voids prior to having her. Even with the blessing of my daughter, problems were still very much a part of my life, but I had tapped into sustaining power from God. Problems were no longer the dominant theme in my life. I threw myself into God, and forced my way into His presence as a coping mechanism.

Family was always a part of my life, but we were divided by states. I was private and didn't believe in sharing my problems or issues with others. Though I spoke to my family daily, I didn't share my personal concerns for many reasons. I guess I acquired that trait from my family. Certain things simply weren't discussed openly.

Marriage was a learning experience. I always wanted to be married, but I quickly learned if I wanted it to work, I had to make major investments. I agreed to make the necessary adjustments and we worked through every issue, and celebrated every milestone. I resolved to not walk away from the marriage at the first sign of trouble. I think it was instilled in me to fight and then fight some more. I learned a lot about marriage as well as about myself, my intolerances, and deal breakers. Most importantly, and though it took years, I learned the true meaning of Unity.

I grew up in a large family but I never needed to be around lots of people. I was content being by myself. I spent so much time alone that it became unhealthy. In shutting everyone out, I was forced to handle all of my problems by myself. My life became a relationship between me and TV's entertainment channel "Life Time." We had many depressing evenings and weekends together. I had to end that relationship and find things that brought me joy.

I was content being home, and loved being a wife and mother. Up to that point, having my daughter was my most fulfilling experience. She brought pure joy to my life. I think I needed her more than she needed me. Even today we have a strong bond. I had no life outside of wife and mother in the early years. Nor was I trying to get a life.

Once I began discovering who I was, I eventually and slowly took my life back by exploring my personal interests and incorporating in my life things that I liked to do without guilt. Little did I know this would be the beginning of me springing forth into who I was created to be. Each outside activity allowed me to walk in greater confidence. I began realizing my potential and abilities.

Participating in school activities and Girl Scouts with my daughter forced me to communicate with others. I was no longer the quiet and reserved Teresa, but I had quickly become publicly known as "Ericka's Mom." Becoming an Independent Distributor of Premier Designs Jewelry was an avenue that took me clearly out of my comfort zone and forced me to fellowship with other positive ladies. It was a business that allowed me to travel to over four states, something I had not done prior to joining.

My writing dates back to elementary school. I wrote letters as a pen pal. I was one who wrote daily letters as family members went off into the military. After high school, I began the journaling cycle regularly. I have provoked and coached dozens of people in writing books. More than half of them will never thank me, but as long as they were obedient to write, God has thanked me.

My English 101 professor was the first person to inspire me to continue writing. She said I had creative style writing. It was years later that I tapped into the fullness of my gift. Writing is therapeutic. It helps to clear my mind, and allows me freedom to be expressive. I don't know what I would do if I could not write.

Next to writing, I operate tremendously in the gift of encouragement. As a child I viewed my compassion as being sensitive to others. I now see it as not wanting to see people stuck, especially when there is another alternative. I have been bound, and I can genuinely say once you are no longer bound, you don't want to see others bound either.

I have a passion for helping others. I provided sound counsel to many of whom were like those ten lepers. Nine of them got what they needed and ran. Afraid to go to their own pastor, they bombarded me time and time again. I dispense all that God gives me, and God rewards me. It's a part of being a peacemaker and wanting to see God's people get what they need to become whole.

I freely give to others. My investment in training others is on a grand scale. I trained those who were as green as celery. Yet when they became partially ripe, they left and never looked back. It's amazing how people serve in churches for years refusing to leave, yet when those same people are called upon to do the basic things in other ministry settings, they are lost. That leads me to believe they are either pew warmers, in hiding or they are not being utilized where they are. Hands on teaching will take you far.

I am an appreciative person. I believe in giving honor where honor is due. Those people who were a part of your life who gave you your start should be recognized. Those who invested in you imparting wisdom, giving of themselves tirelessly need to be appreciated. Treasures are rare, and if you are blessed to have people in your life that helped you along the way, never forget them. In your remembering, let them know you are grateful to them.

I don't shy away from work. I have worked in tobacco, fast food, retail, telemarketing, babysitting, government, and ministry. I have done hard labor and have had desk jobs. At the core of every place of employment, customer service mattered to me. They say the customer is always right. We know that is not true, but the customer is to always be respected, as with the employees and employers. I demand respect because I give it.

I value fairness, and have great respect for those leaders who are fair and equal across the board. I believe in doing good for others when it is in your power to do so. **(Galatians 6:10 NIV, Proverbs 3:27 NIV)** I understand those positions of authority whether abusive or non-abusive. I also understand the wrath of God when abusing authority. My perspective on conflict has changed over the years, I once viewed it negatively. I have heard it said, when you view conflict in the positive sense, you see it as an opportunity to resolve problems.

Sadly, just as much conflict occurs in the church as in the workplace. I used to be content sitting in the back of the church and serving behind the scenes. The same with work, I used to sit in the back of the room at meetings, and I was low key. Today I race to the front of the room in meetings while others flood the back rows. If I am not preaching, I prefer to sit in the front rows at church. Don't mistake any of that for a need to be up front. I can surely play the background.

The fact that I am in ministry is rather interesting in that I never set out to be in ministry. I always wanted to teach, but had no idea I would preach. When I learned I could best help others by sharing my experiences or through relating to experiences, I leaped at the opportunity. I began sharing testimonies, but quickly felt the need to do more. I wanted to be active in helping others, not only grasp what I shared, but I also wanted them to benefit through applying the principles in their own lives.

I am not an education fanatic, though my sister would beg to differ. She thinks I am a professional student. I am far from that, but I strongly believe in being fully equipped. I love to learn but I want to choose the areas that I devote my time to. I chose biblical studies solely because I wanted to be in the word daily. It was a way of forcing me to be diligent. I continued on to the Master of Divinity because God blessed me to skip the bachelor. I opted for the study of Theology because I wanted to know more about God. What better way to learn.

After answering the call to Pastor, and experiencing so many people with so many issues, I felt the need to further my education by incorporating counseling. I matriculated through the doctoral program specializing in Pastoral Counseling. I learned a lot, but because of the vast issues of people, the more I learned, the more I felt I needed to learn. I am always a student with a desire to learn the things of God. I understand the more God teaches me, the more effective I am.

I remember thinking, pastoring a congregation was like talking people off a ledge daily. The difference between police talking them down and me talking them down was, with police some never came off the ledge. Many jumped. With me, they came off, but went back up weekly or monthly. Fortunately, none jumped. I sat on the ledge with many for hours and even in the wee hours of the night.

I came to the realization that warfare is prevalent whether in a Christian setting or not. People are attacked daily. I am no stranger to warfare. The truth be told, every warfare experience prepared me for where I am going. Some things I experienced had nothing to do with me, while other things I endured had everything to do with me. I learned when to fight, and how to fight without getting knocked down or knocked out.

From a child I was known as a peacemaker. I have quieted peace on the inside of me. I don't like confusion, and often I find myself trying to diffuse situations. Years ago I visited family over the holidays. The house was filled with relatives and friends. I walked in not realizing what had taken place short of my arrival.

As I conversed with different family members, I felt the urge to sing some of my favorite up tempo Christian music. I praised from the middle of the floor, until I got caught up. If it's in you, it is going to come out of you. Praise spread as wildfire, as everyone joined in singing.

Shortly after leaving the house I received a call from a young lady. She explained that, prior to me coming to the house; there had been friction among some of those in the house that led to built-up tension. Discord had been sown which caused great anxiety for her and others. Everyone has those relatives who appear to not have filters.

She said when I sang and became very animated in dance, the atmosphere shifted. Everyone joined in singing as smiles swept across the room. These were Christian songs that uplifted me that you wouldn't necessarily hear in church. They were perfect for this setting. When you are being your authentic self, you never know what your presence can evoke. My spirit of peace went into a strained atmosphere and commanded peace. It provoked joy.

The thing about peace is, a situation or circumstance cannot move peace, but peace can always move the situation or cause the circumstance to change. Peace doesn't allow trouble to stay. If trouble comes on the scene, peace escorts it out. I was given peace long ago, and I carry peace throughout my daily walk. It's a priceless and precious commodity.

Because of the "me" I am discovering, I don't have to sit back tolerating every injustice. I no longer want to do nothing about the things that I am passionate about. It feels good to have holy boldness, especially when you have the green light from God.

I started out on this journey with reservations about doing a lot of what I am gung-ho about now. I understand some things will need a special anointing. I use every negative experience and make it pay forward good. I know my contribution is needed in particular areas for breakthrough or to get specific things done.

My journey has taken me far, and higher than I thought possible. My eyes have been opened to many possibilities. Most notably, I am no longer tied to the four walls of my confines. I have been blessed to travel, meet people from all walks of life, and taste a portion of the good life. I have sat with those in high positions of authority as well as with those desiring high positions. I enjoy observing people.

My character has never been to impress others. If I manage to impress them, it's because of who I am and not just what I seek to portray. I don't look for spotlights, but I use those platforms given to me. I am most comfortable sitting back in my reserve state, but I also know how to stand confidently. I am not an extrovert, nor am I an introvert. If I must find a calm balance, it would be that I am an ambivert, which means I can adapt in either state. However, I will not restrict myself to any of those characteristics. I can be whatever God wants me to be on any given day.

I find strength in knowing that God has handpicked me and considered me worthy. Nothing God says has to make sense to me, as long as it makes sense to Him. So you may ask, "Where am I today in the Plan?" My response is, "Freer than I have ever been," "Grateful to be included on such a magnificent, life provoking journey."

Everything that has happened in my life helped to get me to the place I am in today. The bumps in the road, lessons learned were evident, but so were the hedges that stood all day and night waiting to shield and protect me. The growth spurs and all the revelations were working in conjunction to push me to my destined place on time. If God is pleased, then I am overjoyed.

Chapter Two

Vision and Dreams

*"I caused you to see some of what I have for you
And some of where I am taking you"*

Not only does God clue you in on the plan for your life, but He gives you visions. Author Sandy Warner of thequickenedword.com says, "Visions are a special and unique way of hearing from the Lord. Biblical vision is a literal, spiritual and sometimes a physical happening. It's not a product of the mind, imagination or logic. Receiving a vision is a gift from the Lord: an experience of sight, not the imagination." Having a clear picture can take you places you otherwise wouldn't venture to.

Paul says in **Acts 2:17-18 NIV, "In the last days, God says, I will pour out my Spirit on all people. Your sons and daughters will prophesy, your young men will see visions, your old men will dream dreams. Even on my servants, both men and women, I will pour out my Spirit in those days, and they will prophesy."** It is evident to me that God is causing men and women to see visions, dream dreams and prophesy. Of course some are false visionaries, dream killers, and prophet-liars but that's a whole different chapter that I will not tackle in this book.

The Clear Picture . . .

> ➤ *1 Corinthians 13:12 MSG, "We don't yet see things clearly. We're squinting in a fog, peering through a mist. But it won't be long before the weather clears and the sun shines bright! We'll see it all then, see it all as clearly as God sees us, knowing him directly just as he knows us"*

Faith is not about seeing, but seeing causes one to believe. The visions I see come through analogies or what seem like a picture on a movie screen. Sometimes it is as if I am in a dream, only I am awake to witness the entire vision. At the onset of the vision, I screamed with excitement, causing the vision to end. As I matured, I was able to experience the entire vision.

I have accepted preaching engagements where God allowed me to see the faces of the people I am ministering to before arriving. One particular time, I saw a vision of a crowd of about 15 women standing at the altar at the end of service. In the vision I laid hands on and prophesied to those women. When I ministered at the church, sure enough those women came to the altar. It was as though I had already done what I was about to do.

Sometimes I see their faces and other times I don't. I have stood in the mirror the morning I am scheduled to preach and literally seen myself preaching the entire message downloaded by God. At the end I comment, "Lord that was good! Then I ask, "Lord, will you give it to me just like that when I stand before the people today?"

I have been in prayer when God allowed me access to see those people behind closed doors who are grieving. As I watched them from my prayer position, God allowed me to see what no one else could see. The purpose was to intercede on their behalf. I have seen much, which means I pray much. I cannot choose what I see; I can only strive to fulfill what I see.

Some of the visions knock me to my knees in worship. Some cause me to weep with gratitude. Some visions stun me, and others overwhelm me. I don't worry about the results of the visions because in the spirit realm I know they have already occurred. Those visions serve as confirmation to me as to what God will do and how He will use me.

I had visions that provided explanations as to why God allowed a particular thing to happen to an individual, and how He chose to use that person's witness as a result. I have seen mothers with their own children, though they were told they were barren. I saw my dad healed through what's called a "Physical Happening."

My dad was in the hospital with a life threatening condition. The doctors were not 100% confident he would make it through surgery, but there was a chance that he could. I prayed to the brink of exhaustion for him. If I slept, the second my eyes opened, the first words out of my mouth were a plea for God to tell me what He was going to do concerning my dad.

I prayed from my bedroom which was two hours and ten minutes away from the hospital. I saw my dad's body lying in front of me on the bed. The most amazing thing happened where I was allowed to participate in the vision. As I laid hands on dad's stomach, light radiated from his stomach and flowed upward towards the ceiling. I certainly had never witnessed anything like that before. But I can tell you today, just as in the vision; God healed my dad's stomach.

I have a brother that passed at six months old. I did not know him, yet I had an experience where one day it was as if he was looking at me from heaven. He asked me why we never mentioned him, talked about him or acknowledged him. I repented to him and from that day forward I have vowed to acknowledge him in whatever small way I can.

I decided to acknowledge him with the permission of my mother in all of my books along with my other living siblings. I thought another way to honor him would be to include him in the count of how many siblings I have when I talk to others. I have limited information about my brother, but I know he was and is my brother.

Years later, I went to a home going service for a newborn baby. The baby was the grandchild of one of the ministers I served with. There was a brief but precious service held in a chapel. The baby lay in a tiny, yet beautifully made casket proportionate for a baby. The baby was chauffeured by limousine to the burial site; it was less than two minutes away. The committal at the burial site was brief, but it was done as compassionately and professionally as one could ask for.

I don't know what transpired between me walking from the Chapel to the Burial, but while standing at the burial site, I burst into tears. Of course, it was a difficult loss for the family, and I was terribly saddened, but my tears felt over the top for a family I hardly knew. In the midst of my tears, I was learning why I cried uncontrollably. Believe it or not, I was crying for my brother whom I had never met and never grieved. He was a year older than me.

While at the burial site, it was revealed to me that my brother could see me, and he saw me grieve for him. It was the weirdest thing I had ever experienced at that moment. I confided with one of the ministers standing at her car, as I made a mad dash for my car trying to make sense of it all. Her response was along the lines of her understanding what I said happened.

One thing is certain, when I make it to heaven, my brother will know who I am and I look forward to seeing who he is. We are all spirits, and whether we live or die, the spirit lives on forever. You may not recognize the flesh, but you will know them by the spirit. I can imagine he was a cute little thing, full of life until his death. His life touched my life, though it occurred when I was in my early forties.

I had a vision of my coworker Barry sitting on a cloud after his death. I have shared this before, but for the purpose of this book, it is worth sharing again. I say it was a vision, but it was clear as day, and as real as real can get.

Barry had cancer, but it was in remission when I met him. A nice gentleman, focused, mature, and well respected. I never caught him in a bad mood the entire time we worked together. In fact, I made it a practice to share with him much of what God had done for me or was doing. I was a babe in Christ and excited to talk to anyone who listened attentively. Barry listened as if he was intrigued.

For weeks before I really knew he was sick again, I cried weeks on end without fully understanding why I was crying. During this time, my aunt was sick with cancer as well. I was rather invested in praying for them both, and pleaded with God for their healing.

One weekend, I took on some of Barry's sickness. I say that because I experienced a violent wave of sickness without warning. As I struggled through that violently ill period, without going into the details of the sickness, I saw Barry's face.

I believe Barry was relieved that weekend of having to endure the portion of sickness that I took on. I was happy for him, but I vowed not to ever do that again. Taking on the burden of others is no joke. I used to do that with my dad. And I have done that with those grieving. But I have since learned how to quickly put all those burdens back where they belong, off of me.

One day I learned Barry's cancer had returned in a different area. He was hospitalized and had been there a while before I found out.

I asked if I could see him, and was told yes. As I prepared to visit, I was warned that he was on life support. I didn't allow that to crowd my thinking since God was also preparing me. God told me to go and pray the prayer of healing with Barry. I did just that.

It was obvious the nurse wasn't in agreement with Barry walking out of that hospital. Though I'm sure the family wanted nothing more than for him to return to them healed, that wasn't the case. I didn't want them to remove him from life support, but it wasn't my decision to make. I wasn't family and they didn't know me. I am not faulting or judging the family, but at that time all I knew was I was praying a healing prayer which meant Barry would live. I prayed with Barry and I saw him smile though the nurse disputed it. I am confident to this day that he heard me.

When I attended Bible College and Seminary, Professor Graves shared something with me that I hold dearly. My grandmother was in the fourth stage of cancer when I was asked if she wanted to be placed on life support if it came to it. I was devastated to be faced with having to make that decision for her. Professor Graves told me to make the decision I felt was right in my heart, but know that God can override life support if He so desires. Her wisdom made the decision a little easier. Turns out I didn't have to make the decision after all –my grandmother passed.

With regard to Barry, as I left his hospital room, it is obvious now that he was taken off life support. I walked down the hall, still walking in faith, and suddenly I began to double over crying. It was so intense; I was barely able to walk. Using the wall of the hallway to hold me up, I rushed as best as I could to the car where my coworkers waited for me. I was overwhelmed with tears and fought to regain my composure. Not knowing what was really happening, I was a little embarrassed by my uncontrollable emotions.

The last thing I wanted was to return to the car where my coworkers waited and have them see me as an emotional wreck. The moment I reached the car, I looked up to my left and saw Barry sitting on a cloud with his legs crossed. He had his arms folded with his hand positioned on his chin. This was that same position he had when we talked in the office settings.

I screamed with amazement, "Look at Barry!" It took me a while after seeing him sitting on the cloud to understand that when I went to the hospital to pray the prayer of healing, he was healed. Healing can take on many forms, whether here on earth or on the way to heaven. Sometimes God just wants a human point of contact. Not that He needs it, but looking back, I am grateful to have been involved.

God determines what, who and how He heals. I know God could have extended Barry's life well after he was removed from life support. Today I find comfort in knowing Barry was healed. Seeing the grin on his face assured me that he had no complaints. My obedience was necessary whether I fully understood God's plan or not.

As Barry transitioned, the song God comforted me with was, "It is well with my Soul." I thank God even today for allowing me to be a part of such special blessing with Barry. Not just while he was alive, but as he transitioned. Though I miss him, it really was well with my Soul. There will be moments where we experience our true connection with others. Some things are priceless.

What do all these visions do for me? Ignite my faith to higher levels. I believe everything God allows me to see. Vision keeps you going when it seems there is no apparent reason to keep going. Vision comes as encouragement or confirmation. Visions are about God's will and not ours.

Paul had multiple visions during his missionary career. In **2 Corinthians 12:1-6**, Paul had a vision where his body was either in a trance, or his soul was dislodged from his body for a time and taken up into heaven, or perhaps he was taken up soul and body together. While I have the utmost respect for Paul, God is no respecter of person. I am no different from Paul. The only difference I see is, I am alive and he isn't. Unlike Paul, I am still waiting for my vision of heaven. Believe me, I asked to see glimpses of heaven even while I was in air flying to California many years ago. But because God knows me, I wasn't allowed to see Heaven that day.

In **Acts 16:9-10**, Paul went to Macedonia to preach after seeing a vision of a man urging him to come help them. I can certainly relate to that. After seeing myself in a vision standing before women at a retreat, as God would have it, I was asked to be the speaker of a Women's Retreat near Dulles Airport with a two week notice. A young lady who was supposed to be the speaker relocated and urged me to go in her place.

Though there have been many visions, one that stirred me up was when I saw a house on fire, and heard God say to run in and snatch the women out. He gave me the assurance that each time I went in, if I continued to be obedient to Him, He would not allow me to be burned, singed or consumed with fire. That vision gave me the confidence and ammunition I needed to carry out the mission of the women's ministry God allowed me to start.

Years after that vision, the scripture in **Jude 1:23** resonated in my heart stronger than ever. **"Save others by snatching them from the fire."** The vision came before I ever knew about that verse. The point I am attempting to make is the plan for the journey sometimes comes in pieces. When I wrote my first book, I wrote out of obedience. There were things I wrote that I didn't receive clarity from until the second book.

My experience remains, regardless to whether I am ministering to family, a congregation, on the street, in the nursing home, in the work place or in the jail, God remains faithful. If He gives me a vision, that's wonderful. If He gives me a dream, that's great. But I have determined in my heart, despite how the revelation comes, I will represent God to the best of my ability.

In **Acts 18:9-11**, Paul preached in Corinth for a year and six months after a vision from the Lord. God was encouraging him to not be silent and assuring him in the vision that he would not be harmed. One thing is certain, stepping out in faith based on what you believe God is showing you, truly demonstrate an act of obedience. It's an act of boldness driven by faith. Whatever God showed me, regardless to the time frame, if I saw it, I did it or will do it.

Ultimately the clear picture points to every indication of you going into a new direction. However, nothing you did up to this point was wasteful. It was all part of the bigger plan. The same plan that was in effect is still in effect; it's just bigger and more detailed. The mode in which God takes you may be different at times, and the route you take may not look the same as some, but it is necessary in order for so many intricate details to come together.

The Night Vision . . .

> ➢ *Job 33:14-18 KJV, "For God speaketh once, yea twice, yet man perceiveth it not. In a dream, in a vision of the night, when deep sleep falleth upon men, in slumberings upon the bed; Then he openeth the ears of men, and sealeth their instruction, That he may withdraw man from his purpose, and hide pride from man. He keepeth back his soul from the pit, and his life from perishing by the sword."*

Dreams are just as insightful or impactful as visions. It was through a dream that I stepped out to accept my call as Pastor. I remember it like it was yesterday; the message was, "Time waits for no one." I shared this dream before, but it's worth sharing again. There were three barrels set up in an open space and nothing else around. A line of people were preparing to step into the barrels one by one. As each person stepped in they never came back. There were no sounds, no real indication of what was happening.

Suddenly it was my turn to step into the barrel. As I stepped in I began screaming and crying in agony. No! Lord Please! I didn't have enough time! Please Lord! Suddenly I was released and I heard God say, "Time waits for no one!" I woke up shivering and shaking because I knew, though it was a dream, it was real. From that dream on I was determined I was going to pursue exactly what I knew God was saying to do, which was to do the work He was calling me to do right then.

After the dream, when I was finally able to go back to sleep, I did. The next day while at work, going on about the day as usual, I looked in my tote bag for something, only to pull out a piece of paper with the words, "Time waits for no one!" I began shivering all over again. I was shaken to the extent where I had to take action. A dream like that will cause you to run full speed ahead not caring about any obstacles, just fulfilling the purpose for your life.

Just as the vision caused Paul to preach in Corinth over a year, that dream caused me to preach at Bailey Bridge Middle School for two and a half years. Many don't consider the urgency of doing the will of God until it's too late. If I never understood it before, I sure get it now. You think you have time to do the simple things God requires of you. You think you will get around to doing them in your own time. But what if you run out of time and don't do them? Do you believe your excuses will be adequate enough for God?

Dreams can come in the form of a warning, confirmation, or may be prophetic. I have had them all and have benefited immensely. God is able to keep us well informed. He gets information to us regardless to our state of mind. If He doesn't get you when you're awake, He catches you when you're asleep. One thing is obvious; God is communicating more than He gets credit for.

I dreamed I was in another country. I had on navy sports shorts, a white t-shirt with a red stripe and blue tennis shoes almost like cleats. I was running full speed ahead, at a pace where all I could hear was the quick sound of "tap, tap" "tap, tap" as my feet hit the ground. Though I ran fast, I was not out of breath. Alongside me were male lions running at the same pace, in the same direction. Yet they were not chasing me, nor were they bothering me. I had no fear of the lions.

In the dream the lions were an indication that God was with me, and nothing would harm me. When I researched the lion, the revelation I received was, have courage, have faith, stand tall, remember your birthright of power, hold your head high, even in times of conflict, conduct yourself with dignity. **Proverbs 28:1 ESV** says, **"The wicked flee when no one pursues, but the righteous are as bold as a lion."** I realize everything God has proclaimed over my life will be fulfilled.

What I gathered about the dream with the lion was there comes a time when you may have to defend something that is dear to your heart. Just as the lion, defend it fiercely you must. I admit I was in the midst of total warfare. God was showing me in the dream that He was beside me. I had nothing to fear. I ran with the lions. It was time to destroy the works of the devil.

The dream suggests that it was time to show my authority. Not in a dominating way, but through allowing others to still see a loving heart. Jesus was from the tribe of Judah. He is mentioned as the Lion of Judah in **Revelation 5:5**. Jesus, our ultimate example, is full of authority and mighty in Mercy. He lets us know when to sit back and when to fight. Sometimes you have to take a stand, and when you do, God will stand with you. He has you covered when you sleep and when you're awake.

Conducting yourself with dignity when conflict arises says a lot about who you really are. You do not have to succumb to behaving as others. Nor should you allow others to dictate your response. My delayed reaction when thrust into conflict caused me to find a graceful exit.

In school it was said to count to ten before responding to heated situations. Some things happen so quickly you won't have time to count to ten. In some cases people don't respect your space long enough for you to respond appropriately. In the dream, God was giving me the proper response for dealing with what had been inflicted upon me. I took heed.

When someone mistreats you, abuses you or does all manner of evil against you and you take the high road, it doesn't mean that you are weak. It does, however, position you for receiving favor as God judges the situation. The reason being, if God looks at what the person did and sees evil, then He looks at what you did and sees innocence, He is just in favoring you. When your heart is pure and your attitude is upright, whereas you don't do evil for evil nor do you allow impure thoughts and ill motives to contaminate you, God truly has every right to come to your rescue. Give God something to work with.

The Timing . . .

> *Colossians 4:5 AMP, "Conduct yourself with wisdom in your interactions with outsiders (non-believers), make the most of each opportunity [treating it as something precious]."*

I know timing is important and God's timing is everything. I believe I was in place at Bailey Bridge Middle school at the appointed time to reach each person destined to walk through those doors, whether during school hours or after. I believe a hedge of protection was placed around those children throughout the week. We worshipped where they held activities and programs. You cannot tell me there wasn't a residue of the Spirit of God left on those chairs.

Things that typically or randomly happen at other schools didn't happen while we were there.

I watched teachers who came in on Sundays to work, go to the bathroom excessively. Why—because they were listening to the sermon. I saw employees hiding in hallways pretending to work while listening to the sermon. I didn't mind one bit. I witnessed those captivated by the Word but never entered the service. The evidence was the teary eyes we saw as we packed up to leave after service. There were bystanders who gave in and eventually came into the service, while others maintained their distance. That didn't bother me, as long as the Word could be heard.

I took notice of those ministers who said they came to support the ministry but found a place of safety which allowed them to be vulnerable. Leaders often feel they can never let their guards down. As a result of them being so ministry driven, some of them miss their own deliverance. This was a safe atmosphere that allowed them to freely release what they were carrying without judgment.

Those leaders who left their churches for whatever reasons visited and were refueled. There were those suffering from church hurt who didn't want to commit, but they received enough to get them to their next destination. Those who were sick of church came freely and left freely. No one left empty handed. It was obvious what God was doing in these people. God can reach those casual church goers as well as those who want an occasional healing.

Some people have plans to simply pass by. They don't realize in their passing, God is able to make deposits. We don't always know what's best for us. Nor do we always choose the best course. But thankfully, God gets to us exactly what we need. It can be equated to a nutritionist; they have the information that overweight or unhealthy people need, but oftentimes the people aren't ready to receive the information. So they tend to bypass the nutritionist.

Just as the nutritionist has the good, we too had the goods at church, but many weren't ready to receive. Sometimes junk food may appear more appealing than healthy food. People can get so carried away with the restaurant, they accept whatever food is being served. Vegetables may not appear appetizing, but once you start eating them, your body craves them and works a whole lot better for you.

Two different people can preach the same message on the same day, but it comes down to preference as to who you choose to listen to. Just as two people may apply for the same position, they may be equally qualified, but who gets hired may come down to personality. Thank God He has a pastor with a personality and the qualifications to accommodate every one of His children. Unfortunately many are not open to hear where He is leading them. Why stay in a church and be miserable, or with stunted growth.

God knows exactly what He wants to happen and when. One person shared with me how coming to our ministry helped her to expand. She used the analogy of someone incapacitated, bound to a wheelchair for years. She said when she joined, the freedom she had to flow in her gifts as well as some untapped gifts were as if she got her legs back. I certainly witnessed her blossom.

Another person said the teaching was more than they had received over their entire life in ministry. A man commented, had he known church could be this enjoyable and impactful he would have joined years ago. Who doesn't enjoy good teaching? I want to learn, and I want to comprehend what is being taught.

Hoop if you must, but before or after the hoop, give me a Word. Slay me in the Spirit if you insist, but when I get up, I still need a Word. Yell at me if you feel it is necessary, but in your yelling, yell out a Word. Sing to me, "Ain't He Alright" if you have to, but after you're done singing, show me why He's alright. Quote from the internet as you wish, but quote from Scripture as you're required.

Paul resolved to preach Jesus and Him crucified **(1 Corinthians 1:23 NIV.)** You can "Hoop," "Slay," "Yell," "Sing," or "Quote," but I ditto Paul, let it be about Jesus, because of Jesus and for Jesus. I don't proclaim to be the best preacher, or the most thorough preacher, and certainly not the most popular preacher. I gonged in the eyes of others when I first began reading my sermon word for word. I will say I did the best I could when I began. It was thorough and it was truth.

Every preacher should at least consider their audience. Have you ever pondered if half the sermons preached in churches today can be preached in underdeveloped countries? If you stick with Paul's advice and preach Jesus, you can preach that message anywhere.

Getting back to God's timing, He knows where He expects to find you at any given stage of your life. He has a set timeframe to get you there. He knows the pit stops along the way; even the detours because of the choices you make. God lines up people to meet you at every turn. He ensures that the information you need gets to you despite its carrier. Each time you reach your destination, someone else gets their stuff.

Look for every opportunity, seize the moment. In the words of Bishop Robertson, "Meet the opportunity." Don't wait for it to come to you. There are so many things God wants to do and will do, but you must stay alert, in tune, and focused, so that you can take full advantage of the moment.

I worked with a young lady who never spoke to me even if I spoke to her. One day, I noticed something wasn't right with her while in the restroom. When I asked her if she was okay, she responded sternly that she was fine. But I discerned differently and ignored her abruptness. I knew she needed something, and she wasn't revealing anything. I stayed in the restroom and continued to question her. Finally she asked for aspirin or something.

I ran and asked someone else to get the aspirin because I didn't feel comfortable leaving her. She made it to her desk and began crying hysterically. Someone called the paramedics. She somehow ended on the floor. I lay down beside her to calm her and began to pray in her ears. The paramedics came, and I was asked to go with her to the hospital. I could not go but I prayed. Another coworker went with her. Later I received a call asking if I could come pick her up from the hospital. I could not do that either, but I continued to pray.

Time passed and the young lady returned to work. I was so happy for her recovery. When I saw her I spoke, and she once again ignored me. I pressed further asking how she was doing. This time we made eye contact. She said, "You're the one who prayed for me."

Some people aren't used to kindness or intercession, but God places us in position for the saved and the unsaved. I was grateful to God that I could be there for her in her time of need. Her attitude didn't concern me. I was in the right place at the right time, and thankfully I did the work of the Father, which is in my nature to do.

My thanks come from God. Some people will never thank you, but God certainly will.

A man asked if I would come pray a blessing over him. He didn't give me the details but I said yes. He assured me it was most urgent, and contacted me twice to be sure I would come. I knew I was going, but for some reason he needed assurance. I showed up to pray only to find he had convinced others to join us for prayer. He was rather direct in how he wanted the prayer done, and ran to recruit others for prayer just before I prayed. Finally, he turned it over to me. I prayed for him and those he motivated to come. After the prayer they ran, and he nicely showed me the door.

I visited him weeks later. He casually commented that the doctors had attempted to slap cancer on him. He remarked that he had sense enough to call me for prayer. What came out of his mouth next stunned me. He said the results came back with no traces of cancer. I had no clue they thought he had cancer, but the Grace of God intervened.

Though I rejoiced because of God's divine grace towards him, I was also thankful I was obedient and time conscious to handle the request. I did not get a report from the others in attendance in the prayer gathering, but I know the work of the Lord, which says He did something in them and time will tell.

At some point we will face the end of time. Our gift of time is precious. Jesus bought time, but we're living on borrowed time. Some people think they don't have enough time, while others think they have all the time in the world. Each of us are allotted time. Do the work of the Lord. Invest your time wisely.

The Dark Side . . .

> ➤ *Ephesians 5:11 ESV, "Take no part in the unfruitful works of darkness, but instead expose them."*

When I relocated to Virginia, it was nothing short of a move of God. The first day on the job, God told me to see it as an assignment and to be watchful. Some people only see position and salary, but God is about kingdom business. Assignment means there is work to do despite it being the secular workplace. Ministry is 24/7. There will always be someone in need of spiritual guidance, encouragement, and wisdom.

You have to be alert, so that God can show you the things that you may not see. **Ephesians 5:8 NASB** says, **"For you were formerly darkness, but now you are Light in the Lord; walk as children of Light."** When you operate in light, it's like dropping off packages to people. God will show you the need and allow you to deliver the package with what they need inside.

Things tend to hide in darkness, but God is able to expose that which is hidden. **Luke 8:17 NASB** says, **"For nothing is hidden that will not become evident, nor anything secret that will not be known and come to light."** Everything will be revealed. When you have revelation of what you are dealing with, you can channel your energy towards it and target your prayers against it.

Not long after you meet people, God will show you exactly who they are and what their true motives are. Not all people mean you harm, but many are influenced by evil and consumed with evil. It is okay to know you have a Judas in your life. The problem comes when Judas is standing directly in front of you and you cannot identify him. When you know who your Judas' are you know what to expect from them, "Betrayal." When you enter into darkness expect what is dark to appear, but also expect light to override all darkness.

Why do we see so much darkness when we have so much light? **2 Corinthians 4:6 NASB** says, **For God, who said, "Light shall shine out of darkness," is the One who has shone in our hearts to give the Light of the knowledge of the glory of God in the face of Christ."** We do not dispute there is darkness all around. The reason being, evil is ever present. We have all been in some form of darkness at some point in our lives.

Darkness is living in sin without knowing or seeing God. It's stumbling through life operating in unfruitful works with blinded eyes. Those who do not practice the truth walk in darkness. Those committed to darkness ultimately receive judgment as their fate. The blessing is God does not allow you who are light to go into darkness alone.

There is no darkness where light isn't waiting to escort the individual out. **Isaiah 42:16 ESV** says, **"And I will lead the blind in the way that they do not know, in paths that they have not known I will guide them. I will turn the darkness before them into light, the rough places into level ground. These are the things I do, and I do not forsake them."** Whether you willingly walk into darkness or stumble there, God will lead you out if you want to come out.

Why do we spend so much time fighting darkness when our focus is supposed to be on light? **John 8:12 NASB** says, **Then Jesus again spoke to them, saying, "I am the Light of the world; he who follows Me will not walk in the darkness, but will have the Light of life."** Jesus who is the Light will light up your life.

I have worked in many positions, fast food, retail, customer service, marketing, government and ministry. In all of those places there were good people as well as deceitful people. Though the assignment may change with any position, people remain. Everywhere you go, you have to deal with people and master your assignment.

I saw people devoid of God. I heard from the lips of those who casually joked saying they were going to hell in gasoline draws. I saw people who claimed to be Christians but were the front runners for worldly activities and events. I saw needy people, people desperate for positions of authority, people abusive of positions of authority, cut throat people. I saw closet Christians who raced to point out the Christians in the workplace. I saw those who would not take a stand for anything or anyone. I recognized in some there was little to no loyalty to others. Without reservation, I saw wounded people.

It was rather dark and depressing in many ways. It reminded me of high school. I hid in the library during my high school years. I never cared for fighting or the "he said, she said" stuff. I couldn't allow it to affect me. In the beginning of this particular work assignment, I followed suit, as in high school. I hid at my desk behind work for months. I reached a point where I had to do voice checks to see if I could still talk. Just as people do microphone checks, I did throat checks. I did much observing and little talking.

I saw the worst of the organization and the good it offered. There were many good days, but it was for a season. The first few years I walked around grinning, humming and singing. That's because light was shining brightly identifying darkness. Suddenly, dark clouds began developing and the storm headed in my direction. Have you ever been caught in a terrible thunder storm filled with hail, sleet, rain, strong winds, and lightning at the same time? My goodness!

The years of darkness hit with no warning. I have been in many storms, unharmed might I add, prepared for whatever came. Sometimes we get too comfortable and relax our guard because the sun is shining and it's a beautiful day. It's good to enjoy all of that, but we have to be ever learning and ever ready to shift as the need arises.

It was as if I had been thrust into a storm without proper gear, not because I didn't have the gear or didn't weatherproof myself, but because it was my assignment. Some storms catch you off guard without an umbrella, rain coat, rain boots or proper gear, leaving you drenched from head to toe with tree particles and debris wrapped around your ankles. Darkness hovered for a couple of years.

One of the things I did was to determine to enjoy where I was, on the way to where I was going. Because this was an assignment, I could not escape the bad or negative any more than I wanted to exclude the good or positive. I learned to maneuver through the bad days and the good days.

Some days I saw the good in people, as there were good and genuine people there. At times, I had to really look hard to find them, like diamonds in the rough. But just as in any organization, there were also the wounded, misunderstood, the confused and the downright evil. I felt bad for some, compassion for some, and shook my head in disbelief for some.

Soon, most of the people appeared robotic. They went along with the usual routine of stagnation. They were void of voice, and whatever injustices that were done were not their business. I saw people get away with things, and few were punished for their wrongdoing. I saw manipulation, and I saw the hand of God in the midst of the mayhem. Despite what I saw, it was my assignment. Our assignment is to destroy the works of the evil one. It doesn't matter where.

After the years of darkness, the sun began shining brightly through. Shining in a dark place where there is limited lighting isn't always easy, but it is always doable. One thing I learned was, darkness cannot overcome light, but light can overcome darkness. The scripture says in **John 1:5 NLT, "The light shines in the darkness, and the darkness can never extinguish it."** God sends us into areas as light, and we ought to shine as bright as we can. Shine as a child with a broad smile, grinning from ear to ear.

We cannot be overcome as long as we stay connected. **Revelation 12:11 KJV** says, **"And they overcame him by the blood of the Lamb, and by the word of their testimony."** We triumph over darkness by the blood of Jesus and by the bold word of our witness. I was determined to overcome darkness. I went in gung-ho.

Little did I know the fight would quickly turn dirty. I was trying to fight fair, but this devil was hitting below the belt, throwing blows from left field, and just low down and dirty. My husband used to say, "When you're in a fight, you cannot tell the other person what kind of weapons to use." In the natural that is certainly true. I had to step up my fight. I was in a fight with more spirits than I bargained for.

In the spirit realm I thank God He does limit the weapons used. Remember, He challenged Satan to try His servant Job, but He told him that he could not take Job's life? We can go even further with Jesus. Satan tried to tempt Jesus and plotted against Him seeking to kill Him, but in this case, his weapons were not powerful enough to take Jesus' life.

There is a saying among Christians, "Favor isn't fair." I had to quickly get it in my heart and spirit that neither is "Fight." That's because, and I reiterate it's a fixed fight. It was rigged from the beginning for God's children to win. This fight started out with intentions of taking me down but ended up with me fighting on behalf of others. Not everybody wants to fight for themselves, much less fight for others.

At the end of the fight I noticed much of the darkness had dissipated. A lot of those people operating in darkness either left or were driven away. The ones who stayed could no longer straddle the fence participating in evil. They learned lessons of respect in regards to handling God's children. It was as though they were forced to sit on their hands.

When you find yourself in a dark place, do what you were created to do, shine. In dark places you have to leave your place of comfort in order for your true identity in regard to power to be revealed. God is not looking to make you comfortable. Nor is He looking to secure your seat in complacency. When it's time to shine, that means it's time to dispel darkness. You don't go in just for the sake of fighting, but to bring those in darkness to Jesus.

In **Acts 26:17-18 MSG** Jesus says to Paul, **"I'm sending you off to open the eyes of the outsiders so they can see the difference between dark and light, and choose light, see the difference between Satan and God, and choose God. I'm sending you off to present my offer of sins forgiven, and a place in the family, inviting them into the company of those who begin real living by believing in me."** Light is on a mission to rescue darkness, bringing it into the real family of God. Jesus is the first rays of God's daylight shining on people far and near, people both godless and God-fearing. He made us light and activated in us the ability to exude light.

Many times we lose focus reflecting on the dark and we stay in darkness too long fighting and struggling because we tend to take darkness personal. When we stop focusing on the things people are or aren't doing and concentrate on what God is doing or wants to do, we can introduce light. You have to get to a place where you stop allowing the actions of people to derail the real focus, which is getting the people to the light.

The desired goal is to bring those in darkness into the marvelous light of God. You are to convince, motivate and provoke those in darkness to choose light. Ever looked out the window after a beautiful white snow and experienced an almost blinding vision because of the brightness of the sun? Some people have difficulty looking at light; they squint and turn away, but the more they look into the light, the quicker their vision adjusts, adapting to pure light.

There are those fighting through darkness and though it may feel as if they are losing the battle, it really is a fixed fight. If you run towards the light relying on God, you will make it out of darkness every time. God's word truly is a lamp for our feet and a light on our path no matter where we go. **(Psalm 119:105 NIV)**

The Assignment . . .

> ➤ *1 Corinthians 7:17 NIV, "Nevertheless, each person should live as a believer in whatever situation the Lord has assigned to them, just as God has called them. This is the rule I lay down in all the churches."*

Your assignment comes from God. In **John 17:18 MSG,** Jesus said, **"In the same way that you gave me a mission in the world, I give them a mission in the world."** It is not enough for you to merely be God's servant. God has placed you here as a light for others. He expects you take His saving power to everyone on earth.

Each assignment initiates or sets us up to reach the goal of the mission. It's a light mission when you think about carrying out an assignment for the Kingdom of God. As servants we must use out light to carry the message of salvation to the world. The assignment gets us in the door **(Isaiah 49:6).**

In **2 Timothy 1:1-2 MSG** Paul says, **"I am on special assignment for Christ, carrying out God's plan laid out in the Message of Life by Jesus."** Are you on special assignment for Christ? Begin seeing your contribution as invaluable acts. You were chosen among many because you have what it takes to get the job done.

Paul was talking about marriage in this verse, but the concept of assignment can be seen. **1 Corinthians 7:17 NIV** says, **"Nevertheless, each person should live as a believer in whatever situation the Lord has assigned to them, just as God has called them."** Regardless to the task, you have to represent God in a manner that pleases Him. How you carry out the assignment is just as important as the assignment itself.

The assignment before me was rough indeed, and I learned a lot about warfare because of it. Thankfully no assignment will last forever. You go into battle, and you either win or you lose. You should want to win. As soon as you complete one assignment, you move on to the next one. I got some bumps and bruises along the way in completing this particular assignment. I even went a few more rounds than I wanted to in the fight, trying to finish up, but I won. I completed the assignment.

Whatever assignment you may have been given, and despite the location of that assignment, fulfill it. Whether you're in a dungeon or a den, fight your way out. When you come out, make sure you don't come out alone. Bring some folk with you. I can truly say I am stronger as a result. I believe others are closer to God as a result as well. Some were introduced to God.

Now let's be clear, I would not have chosen to go through what I went through, but I appreciate the experience, and it was for a good cause. If God is happy, so am I. He sends His angels to nurse you and tend to you after you have gone through the storm, the dark zone, or the test just as He did with Jesus when He was tempted. If that is not love, I don't know what is. God makes sure we are nurtured and built back up, totally restored beyond where we started.

Timing had a lot to do with the assignment God gave me. I had a previous assignment that turned out to weigh heavily on me because I didn't see how I could possibly fit it into my already overloaded schedule. I petitioned God for the time to complete the assignment and gave Him the specific amount of time I felt I needed. He gave me the exact time I asked for. I realize though I ask and He honors the request, I cannot determine how God gives it to me.

It's funny how one assignment filled with warfare can assist in allowing you to produce in another assignment that's filled with edification. I believe God received glory in both assignments. One was painful while the other was delightful. What I will say is despite what you have on your plate; do not allow time to be a factor in what you do not accomplish. Purpose in your heart to see the urgency of doing what God says.

Expedite every instruction, whether it's to help uplift someone, forgive someone, change your attitude, step out on faith, or fight the good fight of faith. Beware, as it may include destroying the works of the enemy. All assignments are fruitful and have the potential to bring God glory. Some instruction in fulfilling the assignment may seem unrelated, but trust that God incorporates it all. Whatever the instruction, follow it to completion.

I took care of God's business and in return, He took care of mine. I used what appeared negative during warfare to produce what I know is a much needed tool for the body of Christ. **Romans 8:28**

KJV says, **"And we know that all things work together for good to them that love God, to them who are called according to his purpose."** I love the Lord, and I am called to produce in season and out of season. He takes away the excuses that we have and provides a way for us to do what He does daily, "Produce."

Daniel 11:32 MSG says, **"Those who stay courageously loyal to their God will take a strong stand."** In other words, they will do exploits. Make full use of every benefit and resource at your disposal. Be encouraged to stand firm and take action, remaining faithful in every assignment.

Instead of running from your assignment or hiding, run to God trusting Him to help you with it. It's easy to go into shut down mode. And when you operate from your comfort zone, it is easy to suppress issues, or put off dealing with them. Some people compartmentalize their problems to minimize the pain or stress. Avoidance simply prolongs the issue.

God is not like man. He already knows your weakness, and contrary to how man responds to problems, God is constantly equipping, edifying and strengthening you. He doesn't expect you to get everything on your own. He assists you along the way. Every good teacher who gives an assignment explains and clarifies. When you consult with God, He will give you wisdom and revelation. He will help you win.

As hard as it is to hear this, your enemies which reek of darkness help to get you to your place of greatness. They keep you strong in battle. You get where you're supposed to go, and they either get whipped or whipped into shape. It was necessary for Judas to show up on the scene and it is necessary for your Judas' to show up. Jesus knew Judas was coming. So let your enemies come on, but watch how they leave.

The Faithfulness of God . . .

> ➢ *2 Thessalonians 3:3 NIV, "But the Lord is faithful, and he will strengthen you and protect you from the evil one."*

I found out that most people will not take a stand for righteous sake. They are afraid of what they will lose in turn. Jesus had everything to lose, but He took a stand for us and gained everything because of it. People today fear losing their jobs if they speak up about issues of discrimination, racism, or harassment. When they witness unfair treatment, all they concern themselves with is not having others include them.

What I will never understand is how a person can be angry about being mistreated or victimized, yet they will not seek justice; instead they choose to side with the oppressor as if they were never victimized. I watched those who would not stand or compromise their witness for others. When some of the same things happened to them, they wanted sympathy from the very person they shrugged.

People don't always stick around when you are going through your valley experiences. Many have proven to be unreliable. Though many may not have the track record of following through or making good on their word, you can always count on God to stand with you, side with you, and be there for you from beginning to end.

God's word never returns unto Him void. **Isaiah 55:11 NIV** says, **"So is my word that goes out from my mouth: It will not return to me empty, but will accomplish what I desire and achieve the purpose for which I sent it."** That's one word you can trust. When people retreat, God draws closer. When they abandon their commitment, God honors His.

It's easy to trust a God that cannot lie. Each time you witness Him keeping His Word, it builds an even greater trust. Every time you receive manifested promises, it should drive doubt into the ground. The blessing with dealing with a loyal and constant Father is that He never recalls His promise. Nor does He alter His counsel, purpose, or decrees. **Numbers 23:19 ESV** says, **"God is not man, that he should lie, or a son of man, that he should change his mind. Has he said, and will he not do it? Or has he spoken, and will he not fulfill it?"** God never varies in His affections to His people, nor makes void His choice of them, or covenant with them, and His calling of them by His grace.

If you want to be an imitator of God, start with keeping your word. In keeping your word to others, also incorporate keeping the issues and problems of others private. Remember, everything is connected. We really don't have to have an opinion or comment about everyone's business. I personally have enough of my own stuff to occupy my time. So I say to you, Honor God by honoring others.

I have seen so many people comment on the affairs of others, yet they have no back bone when it pertains to coming forward in truth to help those people. One of the many things I admire about God is His consistency despite my inconsistency. **Deuteronomy 7:9 NIV says, "Know therefore that the LORD your God is God; he is the faithful God, keeping his covenant of love to a thousand generations of those who love him and keep his commandments."** God's truth shines light on our affairs. He sets records straight. People, on the other hand, would do well to take cues from God.

When I faced warfare, not only did the demons flee but so did most of the Christians. It is disheartening to be in a battle and have the Christians bail on you. I tell people, when you take a stand, be willing to stand alone. Outside of God, not many will be with you.

I am reminded of Abraham pleading for Sodom in **Genesis 18:16-32 NIV**. He starts out bargaining, asking God, if he could find fifty righteous people, would he spare destroying the city. That number quickly decreased to ten. But God agreed to spare the city for ten righteous people.

Oftentimes people are all over the place, but when you pull out the measuring stick, it's hard to find faithful and righteous folk all over the place. I am so happy that God works with the few He does have. Christians are many until the battle begins. Once the fight starts, they are scarce or should I say, "Scared."

It's good to fight for yourself and your beliefs, but when you venture out fighting for others, you have done something admirable. My husband has gone out on a limb fighting for others many times. It was clear his only motive was to see them get what they so deserved. No matter the result, the fact that you represent someone other than yourself says a lot.

What I like about my youngest brother is, he has said since day one, "Sis, I will stand with you. I have your back. Whatever you want to do and whatever decisions you make, I am with you." He may not agree with everything I say or do but he trusts the God in me and has committed to standing in the gap. He is willing to do the things he feels I cannot do to assist me in getting where I am supposed to go. I don't call on him as much as I could, but at least I know he is there and ready to fight. I can truly say that about all my siblings; they don't all fight the same, but they fight just the same.

Through every dark year of my assignment, God talked to me, provided visions, dreams and positioned people to feed me, nourish me and encourage me. If I became frustrated, He responded to me. If I was discouraged, He sent angels quickly. I was never alone or without hope. I was never without the presence of God. Nor was I ever unproductive.

I don't stop simply because I am hurting, discouraged, disappointed or wounded. I fight when I am well and when I am sick. I cry out to God in good times and bad times. I lean on God at all times.

I know we are troubled on every side, but distress can't hold us down. We are not crushed by our troubles. We are frustrated, and may be unsure about our lives, but we will not give in to despair. We may be bewildered and even confused at times, but God still provides a place where we can be free from disheartenment, hopelessness and desolation. We are persecuted, but we know God will not abandon us. We may be struck down, but we will not be destroyed.

2 Corinthians 4:8 ASV says, "We are pressed on every side, yet not straitened; perplexed yet not unto despair; pursued yet not forsaken; smitten down, yet not destroyed." With every appearance of negativity there is the faithfulness of God, the hope of Glory and the Word of God that drives us to the positive things in life and the good within us. As you can see, we are destined to win.

I resolve to bless God, trouble or no trouble. His praise shall continually be in my mouth. The more the trouble the louder I praise. I yell like a crazy woman, and at the sign of distress, I laugh like I lost my mind. Others may not understand or get it, but I know exactly what I am doing. I am determined to get God's attention and keep it. I don't just want His attention, I want His heart. Deep down I know I have it.

Despite what your eyes see, or your ears hear, you have to focus on what God says and what you hope for. Focus on what you know to be truth. When you know you have previous history with God, you also know you can use it to build greater confidence going forward. The more history, the greater the reliance and dependence should be on Him.

The scripture says it is better to trust in the Lord than to put confidence in man. Oh how much truth is packed in those fourteen words. I shared too much information with a pastor who I thought meant me well. It was after I poured out my heart and later heard from others what I shared in confidence, that I realized she really did not have my best interest. Turns out she was so wounded, that though she initially sought to help me, she ended up wounding me in the process.

Psalm 118:8 AMP says, **"It is better to take refuge in the LORD than to trust in man."** I trusted her to help me at a vulnerable time when ultimately, she needed more help than I did. She started out genuine, but proved to have traits of betrayal. That betrayal wasn't about me; it was about her hurt. I could not remain angry at her because I understood the root cause of the betrayal. I took the high road and chose not to betray her, especially knowing exactly what that felt like.

I am grateful for maturity in the Lord. Regardless to who you are or what title you carry, what's in you ultimately comes out of you. If it were not for God's mercy, and His gracious spirit, who knows what we would do and say on any given day. Sometimes God stands tall in front of us and speaks for us just in the nick of time before we say or do something out of character. I have seen Him do that in my own life, and it is amazing. It's almost like shielding you from a bully or something that you are not strong enough to handle on your own.

Psalm 92:1-4 CEV says, **"It is wonderful to be grateful and to sing your praises, LORD Most High! It is wonderful each morning to tell about your love and at night to announce how faithful you are. I enjoy praising your name to the music of harps, because everything you do makes me happy, and I sing joyful songs."** I cannot thank God enough for the things He continues to do. If you stop and think about what He has done in your life, I imagine you will find yourself in a state of gratitude, overwhelmed and weeping constantly.

The Effective Place . . .

> ➢ *2 Timothy 2:15 ESV, "Do your best to present yourself to God as one approved, a worker who has no need to be ashamed, rightly handling the word of truth."*

Back to the vision and dreams, that dream about time waiting for no one, coupled with the Vision I was given of snatching others from the fire, got me on fire. You can talk a good game and desire in your heart to do much, but until you put your body to action, there is no productivity. There's a phrase, "Action speaks louder than words." **James 2:17 NIV** puts it this way, **"In the same way, faith by itself, if it is not accompanied by action, is dead."** God provides an awesome plan, but you have to get involved in doing the work.

Dr. Myles Monroe said, "The wealthiest places in the world are not gold mines, oil fields, diamond mines or banks. The wealthiest place is the cemetery. There lies companies that were never started, masterpieces that were never painted... In the cemetery there is buried the greatest treasure of untapped potential. There is a treasure within you that must come out. Don't go to the grave with your treasure still within YOU." Determine that you will be effective because God made you to be.

Paul says in **2 Corinthians 4:7 KJV, "But we have this treasure in earthen vessels, that the excellency of the power may be of God, and not of us."** You were made to excel. You have a glorious light that God has placed on the inside of you as a gift to the world. Show the world your gift and allow all those who are supposed to benefit from you to receive from you the portion God has given you for them.

Whatever treasure you house, recognize everything you are able to give to others is a gift from God. Outside of the Grace of God, when people work in their own strength they quickly become exhausted and sometimes depleted. God fills us with all we need when we need it. Every treasure you possess is placed there by God for a reason, to benefit others and to bring God glory.

I will not take my treasures with me to the grave. I realize I will have plenty time to sleep and plenty time to rest, but while I have something on the inside of me, I refused to be idle. I must get it out of me. People often tell me that I need to rest to appreciate my accomplishments before moving on to the next thing. My thoughts are this, I am most grateful to God for all He has allowed me to accomplish whether great or small. I am indebted to God to do my very best in achieving His goals for me. I will rest and I will sleep, but I will not be at peace until I have completed every assignment God has given me.

Everything I have done is the result of a vision, dream or word from God. The wisdom I operate under is "rest when God says rest and work until He says rest." It's not that I am gluten for punishment, or don't have a life or don't want to enjoy life, but I have a commitment to God. I am dedicated to God. I care about the things of God, and I don't want to stifle the treasures I know I have. Because God has given me a gift, I want to make the best of that gift. So if I have to pull long nights to fulfill an assignment while you sleep, so be it.

Some people rest more than they work. They question how you use your time, but they don't use their time wisely. There's a slogan that says, "In the Army, we do more before 9:00 a.m. than most people do all day," and the truth is they do. The soldiers of the military are committed, determined, driven and focused. Christians are soldiers in the army of the Lord. Many of them are committed, determined, driven and focused, and can walk circles around slothful Christians.

There is an imbalance in the kingdom whereas some people are productive and others just are not. Some will work and some won't. I don't want to be in the number of not doing or being willing to do the work of the Lord. I am effective, but I want to be more effective. That only comes through the good and perfect will of God.

Years ago I was in a car accident which left me with multiple injuries. At the time of the accident I heard God say, "Now rest." It wasn't until then that I rested. When I am determined to get something done, there's not much that can stop me or prevent me from working toward it. That drive, determination and motivation came from God.

It's not about busy work; it's about meaningful work that I was given to do. I understand that some things are required and some things are allowed. What I strive to do is the things that are required first, and then follow through on the things that are allowed. Doing it this way brings balance and helps me to maintain balance. Sure, it's more fun doing what's allowed, but if you do what's allowed and run out of time to do what's required, not only is there added stress, but disobedience.

When you do what's required, you will get your time to do what's allowed. Bishop Daniel Robertson once asked this question in relation to vacation, "Why are you taking a vacation if you have not done anything to need a vacation from." There are many people who are tired, but they haven't done anything meaningful. There is a peace and mental fulfillment when you can move projects off your to do list, or satisfy lifetime goals.

Take care of God's stuff and He will make sure you have time to do your stuff. For every weekend you dedicated to nursing homes, jails, evangelism, mentoring or whatever you do, God will reward. It feels good to know you can count on God. Imagine how God feels when He knows He can count on you.

There is so much on the inside of you that you have not tapped into yet. I dare you to dig deeper within. Dr. Myles Monroe said, "You must decide if you are going to rob the world or bless it with the rich, valuable, potent, untapped resources locked away within you." People may admire your tenacity or question it, but your ultimate desire should be to please God with your life. Everything you do should be centered on what God wants. I reiterate, if you do what He wants, you will get what you want. The only time you won't get what you want is when your thinking doesn't line up with His thinking. Getting what you want cannot be detrimental to you or others.

I go to great lengths to get what I need. One morning I fell down thirteen stairs while preparing to go to a Women's conference. I wasn't the speaker, but I was going to support my spiritual mother in the ministry. Though I was in pain and had bruises all over from the fall, I soaked in a hot bath of Epson salt to relieve some of the pain and proceeded to get dressed. I put my heels on and limped on to the conference.

Was it worth the pain? "Yes." The word that was ministered gave me the strength to move through the next chapter along my journey.

I was determined to be at the conference. At the time, I couldn't explain why I still had to be there after falling down thirteen stairs, other than I have great determination. But I have learned, if you feel you need something, sometimes you may have to press pass your circumstance to get it. My toe was broken, but the word helped to heal another area of brokenness I was dealing with.

You will always have the opportunity to use excuses. I guarantee you, something will always occur to make you second guess your decision to do something positive. If you allow excuses, they will show up as if they have an appointment for every engagement you schedule. I decided long ago to shut down all the excuses. I am a woman of my word.

I registered to go to another women's conference. The day of the conference, I began experiencing muscle spasms that caused numbness and excruciating pain. I didn't know what I had at the time, but the symptoms were the worst I have experienced. I pushed with everything in me and went to the conference.

The pain was debilitating. My body began bending at crippling angles throughout my neck, arm, and hand. It hurt to talk, walk and move. I couldn't lift my arm without it feeling as though weights were holding them down. I didn't want anyone to touch me and wished they didn't approach me. My wish was not granted. You certainly cannot expect that in a church filled with women hungry for God, especially when they feel like showing love.

I prayed earnestly to God with urgency as the pain increased. I was literally summonsing God to come to my body immediately. I was assuring Him that I was standing right there in the sanctuary, ready to be healed. No one likes pain but I generally have a high tolerance level. This pain had surpassed labor pains and everything else I experienced. I called God with a 911 request.

During the service, when Pastor Jarvis preached about making a shift, it was as if the Holy Spirit snatched my body. I began worshipping and praising radically (as if I had lost my mind). Every time I jumped, the pain lessened. I jumped, danced and shouted until I could no longer move. Bobby pins flew from my hair and I didn't care. I knew I was in God's presence and He had something I needed. That's desperation.

The next day as I prepared to go back to the conference, I became violently ill with a virus. Not knowing at the time what it was, I went back to the conference. Immediately after the conference, I sought treatment. The reason I pushed is because I knew God was up to something and I wanted and needed it.

God initiated the healing process through my praise and worship. He completed that healing some months later at a "Show me your Glory" Conference. Illnesses were called out and people received there healing. I stood there as person after person testified of their healing. Suddenly, I heard God tell me what to check in regards to my healing. First, He acknowledged my previously broken toe. I wasn't able to bend my toe after breaking it, until this conference. I happily received healing.

Then God said to check my arm and hand where the muscle spasms were. At that time, if I closed my left hand allowing my fingers to rest on my palm, my fingers went over board and latched onto my wrist refusing to let go. It was painful and had the appearance of deformity. I thought to myself as God said to check it, "Lord if my hand isn't healed, you're going to have to pry if from my wrist and I'm going to scream out loud."

The thing is, either you trust God or you don't. Your faith grants you access to total healing, but your obedience brings about the healing much faster. I checked my arm and hand, and praise the name of Jesus I was healed. The process for my healing began in April and was completed in September. Wherever God begins, just know He will also bring an end.

I went to Physical Therapy and was told that this type of pain comes on as a result of stress. I am secure in my healing, but wisdom says regardless, monitor the stress. Stress was accustomed to hanging around. However, the more I learn about God, the more I realize how capable I am of removing the stress. I don't have to allow stress on board each time it feels like going for a ride. If I put stress in check, it won't show up in some other form.

If you want God to utilize you, you have to remain in an effective state. How do you do that? By taking care of yourself and doing what God says as it relates to your health and your body. I want to remain in an effective state so that God can utilize me. I don't want Him to call on me to do a thing and I respond I can't do it.

When I received my total healing, others witnessed God at work. Soon after my testimony, there were other testimonies of healing in the same area. When I am obedient to tell all God has done or is doing, it impacts others. Some people will grow in faith as a result of your faith. Your testimony is more effective than you realize.

In the bible, testimonies became contagious. The more God did, the more people told what He did. And the more the people told, the more God did. You do not have to share from a bull horn, but you should tell about the goodness of God in your life. He plans to do even greater things than you have seen this far. I don't know about you, but whatever He does for me, I will surely tell. One reason being, I am grateful that God is at work in me. I appreciate the work He does for me.

The Evidence Speaks for Itself...

> *Ephesians 3:14-20 NIV, "For this reason I kneel before the Father, from whom every family in heaven and on earth derives its name. I pray that out of his glorious riches he may strengthen you with power through his Spirit in your inner being, so that Christ may dwell in your hearts through faith. And I pray that you, being rooted and established in love, may have power, together with all the Lord's holy people, to grasp how wide and long and high and deep is the love of Christ, and to know this love that surpasses knowledge—that you may be filled to the measure of all the fullness of God. Now to him who is able to do immeasurably more than all we ask or imagine, according to his power that is at work within us, to him be glory in the church and in Christ Jesus throughout all generations, for ever and ever! Amen.*

Obedience and discernment can take you far. I was told when you have a vision that benefits, encourages or warns someone else and you don't share it beforehand, you are not allowing God to get glory. A coworker used to share her dreams with me after an incident had already occurred. I told her though I believed her; anyone can share a dream after the fact and claim it to be so. I encouraged her to share it before it happened so God could get glory and so she could receive confirmation.

That leads me to a young lady who lost her oldest son in a very tragic accident. I woke up after midnight with an unusual prompting to check my email. Upon reading the email with the news that her son was killed, I began praying. All I could think of was the grief she must have been experiencing. While praying, I initially saw her and two other people standing together crying. Then I saw one person holding on to her trying to pick her up as she was quickly falling to the floor. My heart ached for them as I prayed intensely.

Sometime later, after talking to her, it was confirmed that she was standing in the hospital with her husband and younger son when she received the awful news that her oldest son had passed. She said she literally fell to the floor when she heard the report from the doctor. Her youngest son was holding her, trying to pick her up as she was falling to the floor.

Some visions aren't pretty, and of course I didn't get any joy out of that confirmation of my vision, but I found peace in knowing that my prayer was on target. I thank God we are able to connect with others and intercede without being present. I don't believe God shows everyone visions of such magnitude, but I am glad He trusts me enough to show me the ones He does show me. It comes back to the word, "Connection." We are all here to work together toward a common purpose, the Kingdom.

There are times when you will see things outside of visions or dreams, literally happening in front of your face. I have seen indicators of sin in people who are dear to me. As a result, I go into battle coming against what I see that is wrong whether I have the full details or not. When my spirit is annoyed because of the wrong I see, I begin praying. I may not tell you that I am praying, but sooner or later, you will know that I am.

I was called "Thunder" early in ministry. That classification of me simply alludes to my nature being that of a loud rumbling or crashing noise. It is good to make a loud noise, but it is better to be effective as a result of the loud noise. It was recent that I was described as "Quiet

Storm," meaning, it may not be evident at first, but I am capable of manifesting a great disturbance in the atmosphere, with strong affects. It can be viewed as doing much damage in the Kingdom of darkness.

James 5:16 NIV says, **"The prayer of a righteous person is powerful and effective."** I know the power of my prayers. Luckily for some, I don't use them as David did in **Psalm 109:8-13**. David was honest in his prayers. Me on the other hand, I try to remain silent opposed to asking God to take folk out when they do me wrong. David cried out for vengeance. I reached a point where in my heart I decided I would cut my enemies off from showing them mercy. I remember feeling victimized all over again when someone aware of the injustice I experienced asked me to show my enemy mercy.

My issue was I prayed for them when they were in need. I supported them in every way I possibly could, yet they sought to destroy me. They attempted to discredit my witness without cause. My character was on trial. I had major issues with that.

David said in **Psalm 109:1-20 KJV, "Hold not thy peace, O God of my praise; for the mouth of the wicked and the mouth of the deceitful are opened against me: they have spoken against me with a lying tongue. They compassed me about also with words of hatred; and fought against me without a cause. For my love they are my adversaries: but I give myself unto prayer. And they have rewarded me evil for good, and hatred for my love."** I prayed for my enemies more than I prayed for myself earnestly, yet they plotted against me, schemed and lied. They didn't care about the suffering they caused me. Yet I should care about their suffering as they faced punishment for evil treatment towards me.

David said, **"Set thou a wicked man over him: and let Satan stand at his right hand. When he shall be judged, let him be condemned: and let his prayer become sin. Let his days be few; and let another take his office. Let his children be fatherless, and his wife a widow. Let his children be continually vagabonds, and beg: let them seek their bread also out of their desolate places. Let the extortioner catch all that he hath; and let the strangers spoil his labor. Let there be none to extend mercy unto him: neither let**

there be any to favor his fatherless children." David wasn't playing with his enemies, just as his enemies were not playing with him.

Some people take Christians to be weak with no back bone. Pardon my French, but being a pastor does not mean you are a punk. Nowhere in ministry have I seen a permit given for Christians to be used as floor mats or trampled upon. Like David, I will not lie down and die, nor will I roll over and play dead when the enemy approaches me. I do not start fights, but I will fight making my enemies wish they never started them.

David was a prayer warrior, but he was also a man of action. Action really does speak louder than words. The enemy will have a field day with you if you allow him. Don't take chances with him. And certainly don't let him get away with anything. Make him pay every cent he owes you and for every wrinkle he causes to rest on your forehead.

I was told that my prayers caused many things to shut down. I have even been asked to stop praying. I cannot pray an impure prayer because I am not talking with man; I am talking with a pure God. I cannot manipulate God, but I can go to Him and reason with Him about what bothers me.

Some people are happy in their sin. Some feel they cannot survive without the practice of sin, they see it as a means for their livelihood. My response to those people is, "If I am on assignment to cover you in prayer, do not allow me to boldly see your wrongdoing." Otherwise you leave me no choice than to pray shutting it down, especially when it's wrong.

1 Thessalonians 5:22 AMP says, "Abstain from evil [shrink from it and keep aloof from it] in whatever form or whatever kind it may be." Some people think you are naïve to their sin. In one particular case, what I saw was the appearance of evil and not just by my standard. Just because an individual refuses to abstain from evil doesn't mean you have to go along with it. The fact that a thing was done in your presence, while you have a connection to the person, gives you the authority to come against what you saw. We don't have to get permission to pray for people, but when a person has asked you to pray for them, you are free to pray for the will of God to be done in all areas of their life. It's all for their good.

1 John 3:8 MSG says, **"So, my dear children don't let anyone divert you from the truth. It's the person who *acts* right who *is* right, just as we see it lived out in our righteous Messiah. Those who make a practice of sin are straight from the Devil, the pioneer in the practice of sin. The Son of God entered the scene to abolish the Devil's ways."** If Jesus appeared for the purpose of destroying the works of the devil, and we are His disciples, then we too are here to destroy the works of the devil.

As I reflect on the dreams I have had, some were astonishing. Of course, there are some dreams that others will never understand; maybe that's why they weren't the ones having them. As long as what God is saying is being fulfilled, that's where my faith resides.

I had dreams regarding warnings, as well as the responses to a word of warning I am led to give. My dreams come to pass despite the "woe unto you" warning in some cases. In other cases, the people take heed and what was going to happen is cancelled. Praise God! Just like with the Prophet Jonah and Nineveh, the people listened and turned from evil, and God responded positively. He relented and did not bring on them the destruction He had threatened **(Jonah 3:3-10 NIV.)**

One dream I had was where two people were in violation of a particular thing, yet they continued to violate the very thing that got them in trouble in the beginning. They didn't want to suffer the consequences, but they were not doing anything to avoid the consequences. In the dream, they both were caught and facing punishment for the same thing. I cried and was heartbroken in the dream. When I woke up devastated, I called both people to warn them. One was in denial. The other person chalked it up to me simply having a bad dream or being paranoid.

Later I received a call from the person who was in denial, confessing the dream was real and the punishment was already in effect. Dream or no dream, it hurts to see someone suffer. No one wants to see a negative dream come to pass. At that point, all I could do was pray for the most positive result possible for the person. I am still praying for the one who brushed me off as if I was paranoid.

I used to keep dreams to myself, but when it's a warning, I consider sharing them. If the dream is one of those private issues that could prove harmful, I pray to God to cancel out what I saw. That's called dismantling things of darkness before they even occur. God shows us things for reasons. When you see things that you know are not right, start praying.

The majority of my dreams have ignited a fire within me, provoking me to action. Some dreams have shown me how powerful the anointing on my life is. Some have revealed to me my ability to fight and war in the spirit even while I sleep.

A lot can happen in a dream when you are asleep. Sometimes, whatever weighs heavily on you can find its way in your dream. Your conscious can release things in your sleep. Sometimes whatever is on T.V., when you fall asleep, can creep into your sleep. Then there are those dreams where God reveals things to you.

Some dreams are loaded with temptations. When it comes to dreams, be aware that not all dreams are from God. Above all, even with dreams, be sure you place your hope and trust in God and not in the dream.

The good news about most of my dreams is that regardless to what they are, I pass the test in the dream. I believe if you can pass the test when you're subconscious you can certainly pass the test when you're wide awake. At one time, I asked God to stop the dreams so I could rest. Today, dream or no dream, I cling to the words of David in **Psalm 4:8 ESV, "In peace I will both lie down and sleep; for you alone, O LORD, make me dwell in safety."** When you know God is with you and for you, you do not have to fear what comes in daylight or nighttime, in visions, or dreams.

I recall the situation between Joseph and Mary. Joseph had a lot to deal with when Mary appeared pregnant. He knew he wasn't the father. Thank God for dreams and visitations. Personally, I have prayed that others have dreams revealing truths to them in unrelated areas.

Matthew 1:18-25 ESV talks about the birth of Jesus. **"Now the birth of Jesus Christ took place in this way. When his mother Mary had been betrothed to Joseph, before they came together she was found to be with child from the Holy Spirit. And her**

husband Joseph, being a just man and unwilling to put her to shame, resolved to divorce her quietly.

But as he considered these things, behold, an angel of the Lord appeared to him in a dream, saying, "Joseph, son of David, do not fear to take Mary as your wife, for that which is conceived in her is from the Holy Spirit. She will bear a son, and you shall call his name Jesus, for he will save his people from their sins." What a tough pill to swallow. Many things occur today that some have not found peace with. Not everyone who wrestles with finding truth finds the real truth this way. But what an amazing confirmation Joseph received, all in an effort to fulfill a prophecy.

Imagine all the things God has spoken over your life that shall come to pass. He goes to great lengths to make sure His word is accomplished. Sometimes in life you need vision and dreams just to make it through. They can be what cause you to cling onto your faith at a time when you need it most. I have asked God on occasions to reveal truth to those who have persecuted me. I believe He did in some cases.

I had a vision of a young lady making a huge scene as she persecuted me openly before others. I could not hear her conversation about me, but I saw her body language, and I knew her foul language as she was accustomed to using on any given day. I was surprised to be a recipient of the persecution, but I wasn't angry because I viewed her as harmless. She had a big bark but no bite. I didn't waste my energy on pursuing it, but I was full aware.

Can God trust you with what He shows you? How do you handle what you see? Not everyone is receptive to your dreams. I believe sometimes it can be rather embarrassing for a person when they realize you have been included in something that involves them. But the dream is not for you to have something to hold over someone's head.

I shared another dream that I had with a young lady. I was a little uncomfortable doing so considering it was about her. I took into consideration how I would have felt. Through talking to her, it was confirmed that the dream was accurate but there was one thing fuzzy in detail. She clarified what was fuzzy. I learned that sometimes God may allow you to see something that's in the ball park relating to a subject, but He may not give you the specific thing.

My only motive for sharing the dream with the young lady was because she shared in an open conversation with me and others something that pretty much alluded to what I saw in the dream. I had resolved to pray and not speak on it. My only intention after having the dream was to stand in the gap interceding for her.

This next dream is on the other end of the scope. To me this dream showed how God will prepare you to receive bad news. I dreamed that our grass had gone from a healthy beautiful green color to a brown, the color of straw or hay overnight. In the dream I woke up and looked out the window at what we once knew as grass so thick that it felt like plush carpet. The grass was so green, it was as if we had colored it. It was so appealing to the eye that neighbors stopped and stared. My husband had worked so diligently weeks on end with upkeep.

In the dream the grass had turned brown, almost resembling the residue of a forest fire. I screamed as I looked at the death of the vibrant green grass. When I awakened and looked out of the window, the grass was still green. I was relieved. Not long after, I looked out the window and sure enough the entire backyard was filled with brown grass. It was as if something sucked the life out of our grass. Though it was painful to see, the dream softened the blow.

That summer there was such a drought, it spread across the neighborhood. Practically everyone's grass was brown. I don't know if we could have done much else to get a different result.

My Response to the Vision and Dreams . . .

> ➢ *Ephesians 3:7 NIV, "I became a servant of this gospel by the gift of God's grace given me through the working of his power."*

I go to great lengths to bless others. I endeavor to fulfill every vision God gives me. Some of them that I will not speak of in this book are pretty life changing. If I shared at least one of them, some people out of jealousy would probably want to push me down an empty cistern as Joseph's brothers did to him. You cannot successfully imprison what God deposits into His people. Joseph may have been thrown into a pit, but His dreams were still very much alive and active.

I welcome visions and dreams from God. I generally work pretty quickly to fulfill the vision. I cannot say I have fulfilled them all, but I can say I have attempted. This is a limited list, but some things I did quickly to fulfill a vision were: answer my call, get in position, help someone get out of trouble with the law, preach a message, speak at retreats, start a ministry, give away furniture, purchase a ministry van, cross the finish line in graduate school, encourage those grieving, prophesy to others, prepare for a promotion, prepare for a vacation, warn others, sow seeds, reach out to others, step out on faith, and pray intensely.

I gained confidence like never before as a result of the visions. I have vision because of the visions. The fact that God has revealed to you that He has a plan for you, and has given you visions and dreams lets you know that He is not hiding anything or withholding anything from you. Not His plan, nor His Vision or Dreams. His word says in **Psalm 84:11 NLT, "For the Lord God is our sun and our shield. He gives us grace and glory. The Lord will withhold no good thing from those who do what is right."** When you walk upright, living with integrity, God will not deny you any good thing. He gives you favor and honor. That's nothing short of His undying love.

Helen Keller said, "The only thing worse than being blind is having sight but no vision." People may attempt to minimize or shrink the vision by telling you what you see won't work, or what you see isn't possible, but you must press on. Some people want to limit your thinking and productivity because they haven't faced their own realities. Having no vision is the same as having no hope or confidence. Don't be caught without vision.

When I accepted my call to preach, I shared it with a young lady who said, "No, I don't see that, I see you teaching." It wasn't about what she saw; it was about what God knew. However, turns out she did have partial vision. I am a preacher who teaches.

It's a blessing to be able to see. Johnathan Swift says, "Vision is the art of seeing what is invisible to others." We were all blind at one time or another, but God has graced us to see. You must remember, people didn't cause you to have vision, and people should not be given that much power over you as to cause you to forfeit the vision. Be obedient to carry out the vision and live out the dream. Your obedience will bring to pass the vision or the dream.

Leroy Hood says, "Don't underestimate the power of your vision to change the world. Whether that world is your office, your community, an industry or a global movement, you need to have a core belief that what you contribute can fundamentally change the paradigm or way of thinking about problems." You have been given treasures in visions and dreams. Each treasure is to be used to bring forth even more treasures. Put your treasure to work.

The treasures I have been blessed with have blessed many. I don't say that in a proud way to highlight my good, but I say it in a boastful way to highlight the Glory of God. God has allowed me to reach masses of people from all walks of life. Some of which I experienced long drawn out conversations with while others were only split seconds. My life has purpose and meaning. God meant to create me for His good purpose. I plan to live up to His expectations of me in a good way.

Joel A. Barker says, "Vision without action is merely a dream. Action without vision just passes the time. Vision with action can change the world." You were created to be a part of change. Push the vision, live out the dream, and move expeditiously in the plan of God.

In my case, visions and dreams allowed me to see what was to come. Much of my inspiration is a result of what I have been shown, but the majority of what I do is due to what I know about God. The more I know about Him, the more I want to know. Knowledge of Him increases my drive, motivation and passion. I am not satisfied with the norm. The more I see, the greater my expectations.

I am in total agreement with Paul when he said in **Ephesians 3:7-13 MSG, "This is my life work: helping people understand and respond to this Message. It came as a sheer gift to me, a real surprise, God handling all the details. When it came to presenting the Message to people who had no background in God's way, I was the least qualified of any of the available Christians. God saw to it that I was equipped, but you can be sure that it had nothing to do with my natural abilities.**

And so here I am, preaching and writing about things that are way over my head, the inexhaustible riches and generosity of Christ. My task is to bring out in the open and make plain what God, who created all this in the first place, has been doing in secret and behind the scenes all along. Through followers of Jesus like yourselves gathered in churches, this extraordinary plan of God is becoming known and talked about even among the angels!

All this is proceeding along lines planned all along by God and then executed in Christ Jesus. When we trust in him, we're free to say whatever needs to be said, bold to go wherever we need to go." We see evidence of God's power, and experience His Glory because of His mercy and Grace, but also because of our trust in Him and obedience to His Word.

Paul says he became a servant of this gospel by the gift of God's grace given him through the working of His power. God certainly works through His servants in mighty ways. I am glad to be counted among the faithful and honored to have received such gift of Grace.

Chapter Three

The Call: Destiny for You

"Your call is bigger than you realize"

Ever wonder why you go through all you go through? Sometimes it is because of the call on your life. Years ago a prophet told me, "If you want to be a pioneer, you have to do pioneer things." Whatever you are called to do, you will also have to do the things required by God to get to the place He has called you to. I don't know one doctor who didn't study about medicine. I don't know a construction worker who isn't either skilled in trades, operations or as a general worker. Nor can I point you to one Beautician who doesn't know how to apply chemicals. Whatever your call, it should be perfected. There will be work you will have to do to participate in the call.

The call on your life is about your past, present and future. Where you are going is far greater than you can see or imagine when you first accept the call. God gradually unfolds the call to you. For some it starts at a young age, for others it may be fast paced, but nevertheless the call is spread out. Meaning when you learn of the call, you don't jump to the end of the call. You start at the beginning of the call and work your way through.

Did you know you can operate in what you know to be your calling, but still not be operating to the full extent of that call? Jesus began operating in His call, but later demonstrated the full extent of the call. He did that over a period of thirty-three years. As a child there were things He noticed but didn't understand. As a teen there were things He did but didn't understand. As an adult He ran full speed in the knowledge of what God had for Him to do without question.

He was called to save the world. Though He could have, He didn't start off saving the world. He started off living in the world that needed to be saved. He experienced the world and was able to be an example among the world. He walked out every example we would ever need. He was the living epistle who paved the way for other living epistles to come.

Jesus knew what it was to be embarrassed, humiliated, crushed in spirit, and brutalized. He knew before the cross, on the way to the cross and while hanging on the cross what persecution, rejection, and abandonment felt like. His call was demanding and required suffering. In life your call may get ugly, but trust that it is worth the effort. Fight your way through with the goal in mind to please God. Just as Jesus didn't choose His call, neither did you.

The physical side of the call was challenging for Jesus, but He maneuvered through each challenge. The spiritual side of the call was life provoking, and He provoked lives every step of the way. While on the cross lives were saved. Hearts were convicted, and minds were transformed. You should be driven to provoke good while impacting lives.

Despite the challenges, there were parts of Jesus' call that were good. Imparting truth and knowledge to His disciples must have been satisfying. Sure it must have felt good raising Jairus' twelve year old daughter and Mary and Martha's brother Lazarus from the dead. Standing against judgement for the woman caught in adultery, and healing the woman who touched His garment had to be rewarding. Not to mention feeding thousands, and showing Peter what it took to walk on water.

Though Jesus carried out every aspect of His call to the satisfaction of God, He didn't do it all at once. Jesus' call was gradual in that He didn't step into all of the duties of the call immediately. Not that He was a procrastinator, but instead He did all things timely to fulfill the Will of God.

At age twelve Jesus visited the Temple in Jerusalem. Between ages twelve and thirty Jesus worked as a carpenter in Nazareth. At age thirty, Jesus was baptized in the River Jordan in Judea by John the Baptist. He went into the wilderness in Judea, turned water into wine, and drove out the moneymakers from the Temple. Jesus visited Nicodemus, talked to the Samaritan woman, and performed a miracle at Cana in Galilee. He healed at the pool of Bethesda, and read in the Nazareth Synagogue.

At age thirty-one Jesus preached and taught His Sermon on the Mount. He healed the Lepers. At age thirty-two Jesus didn't just read in the Nazareth Synagogue, but He taught there. He provided the miracle of the loaves and fishes in Bethsaida. Jesus walked on water, and He foretold His Own fate. At age thirty-three, Jesus dealt with betrayal, went through the Garden of Gethsemane, trial, crucifixion, resurrection and ascension.

This is not all Jesus did, but it is a lot of what He was sent to earth to do. Jesus was on a timeline, and He completed it at age thirty-three. Believe it or not, you have been given a timeline too. I cannot tell you when it ends, but I can assure you it will end. Jesus made His time count. You don't have to go through life so serious that you can't smile or stop saying hallelujah thank you Jesus long enough to converse with others, but you do have to make the most of your time. You don't have to race through life afraid you won't get everything done, while missing out on what is important, but you do have to live life wisely.

Every call comes with a cross. If there is no cross, there will be no crown. Just as you cannot exclude the call, you cannot overlook the cross. Unfortunately, you don't choose the call, neither do you have a say in the cross. It's as simple as this, "Accept the Call, Carry the Cross, and Receive the Crown." Or you can "Reject the Call, Neglect the Cross, and Forfeit the Crown."

The Importance of Your Cross . . .

> ➤ *1 Corinthians 1:18 KJV, "For the preaching of the cross is to them that perish foolishness; but unto us which are saved it is the power of God."*

One of the things that stood out to me is that the cross was an avenue for all to sit at the feet of Jesus. The cross worked to command an audience for Jesus. Though it was traumatic, the cross provided an opportunity for Jesus to be where He was destined to be and still reach others. What can be more fulfilling than to sit at the feet of Jesus? Souls were saved while He hung on the cross. Lives were transformed from the cross. People recognized He was the King of Kings and Lord of Lords as a result of the cross.

The cross reveals to us the character of God. It brings us to the Father. His love for lost sinners and His perfect justice meet at the cross. The cross is the intersection of God's love and His justice. God's goal was to show us His love for us. He did that. The cross meant life, not death. It meant love rather than hatred. It provided direction and clarity for us.

Jesus knew that since our problems stem from sin, the solutions to our problems must be centered on the cross. He went to the cross knowing full well it was a place where all the wounds of sin could be healed. His goal was to show us God. He did just that. He honored God always, but especially while carrying His cross and while hanging on the cross.

1 Peter 2:21-25 MSG says, "This is the kind of life you've been invited into, the kind of life Christ lived. He suffered everything that came his way so you would know that it could be done, and also know how to do it, step-by-step. He never did one thing wrong, Not once said anything amiss. They called him every name in the book and he said nothing back. He suffered in silence, content to let God set things right.

He used his servant body to carry our sins to the Cross so we could be rid of sin, free to live the right way. His wounds became your healing. You were lost sheep with no idea who you were or where you were going. Now you're named and kept for good by the Shepherd of your souls." What better Overseer of our souls than God? He is the Bishop and the Guardian of our souls. Jesus did the unimaginable for us.

Jesus showed us step by step how to trust God to be at work in our situations. God works behind the scenes before we can ever see Him at work. He worked behind the scenes at the cross. Love poured out its greatest measure from the cross in numerous ways: through forgiveness in those who wrongly crucified Jesus; provision for His mother Mary and His friend John; life in the criminal nailed beside Him; inner strength as He Himself thirst to do His Father's will; total reliance as He felt the sin and weight of the world; connection as He joined Graces with His Father after thirty-three years; and fulfillment as He conquered the world and pleased His Father.

We can see the full fruition of His plan of the cross today, but it was not evident to all at the time. It's amazing how we get to look back and benefit still. The significance of the cross is not to say that it was the end for Jesus. In fact, the cross points us to an empty tomb, which says not only is Jesus alive and well, but He created that life eternal for us as well.

You have a cross and you have destiny. Before birth, God emerged you into His good plan, purpose and will. Some days it may seem as though you have it hard, and other days it may be that you have it easy, but all days are of equal importance. With the same enthusiasm you have on the good days, you will need on the not so good days.

Ever seen someone put their lives on the line for a cause? Many of them are on the kingdom team. People who are called to advocate for others are most compassionate about what they do. The most passionate and compassionate one I have knowledge of is Jesus. There were many forerunners who ran full speed with a kingdom agenda. I would rather be among those runners than to be in the number of those backsliding.

I experienced hardship, grief, and the list goes on. I also was privileged to experience wealth, prosperity and blessings, and that list goes on. All of those experiences were relevant. All of those ordeals and successes helped me in reaching others. I didn't want my cross until I began seeing the cross others carried. After seeing some pretty devastating crosses, I ran back and pleaded for my cross. I felt, my cross I could easily bear. I thanked God I didn't have the cross many had.

I am overly grateful for many things. To name a few, I was born into a society that preaches Jesus. I could have been born anywhere never hearing of Jesus until some missionary came through. I can pray, worship, praise, evangelize, read, preach and teach freely. Some are in danger of doing the very thing we take for granted.

I can eat as many times a day as my stomach will hold food, yet others starve. I remember eating mustard sandwiches and going as far as eating from the trash can. In the early years, nine of us shared one bathroom, now three of us have three individual bathrooms. Even greater than that, I can worship freely, sit where I want, and vote if I choose to. Though I am female, I can voice my opinion, while many are treated as though they have no voice and forbidden to speak. I don't have to be forced into marriage, fearful of abduction or threatened by abuse, but there are those who live in fear or bondage daily.

With those things alone, that should be enough to cause anyone to jump at every opportunity God gives. Yet when God asks us to do the simple things, we are shrug with hesitance. Jesus was eager to glorify God. You can clearly see the impact of Jesus' cross. Had He not carried His cross, you and I would not be having this conversation. Think about how many conversations will be had because you carry your cross. His cross had everything to do with you. Will you make your cross about everyone else instead of you?

When I think about the importance of what I do for the Kingdom, it overwhelms me to tears to do anything but what I do. I cannot say no to God. I have learned how to say no to man, but there is nothing God will ever ask me to do that I will not do. I have done things for God and cried while I did them, just as I have done things walking scared, but I did it. My only request was that He was with me, and never left me. He lived up to His end of the bargain as did I.

Some people come to earth with a call on their lives and live well into their 90's or 100's, while others go as far as their teen years and sometimes just after birth. Regardless to the time span, everyone is called onto earth to do something that fits in the plan of God. And despite what we think, people accomplish the call they were sent to earth to accomplish.

It's obvious that Jesus lived out the call on His life. But sometimes it may not be as easy to see as it was with Jesus. Let's take Lucifer for example. He was created to guard the very throne of God. He was perfect in wisdom, beautiful beyond description, a magnificent musician and held the highest exalted position. He did just what he was created to do. Now, what he did afterwards was another story, and what will happen to him as a result is a different story. But I would venture to say God got out of him what he intended to get out of him initially. His first call was to guard the throne. God never loses. He gets out of you what He puts in you.

Though God wins with what He created Lucifer to do, it was Lucifer who stepped outside of the will of God and as a result, was kicked out of heaven. Now he is serving a death sentence without parole. He is a defeated foe and he knows it. Had he not become prideful and evil, his destiny could have been different. One thing for certain is, if I ever step foot in heaven, I'm sure not going to jeopardize staying there. And while I'm on earth, I am going to fight daily to ensure I make it to heaven.

Jesus came to earth, walked the earth and made it His business to do all God told Him to do on earth, in the tomb and even in hell. From the wilderness to Gethsemane to the Cross to the grave, He complied with God. It wasn't optional with Jesus. He sought to please God, and God was well pleased. The bottom line is Jesus showed us how to work the middle as God finishes the work He starts. God doesn't ask you to start the call, nor does He ask you to finish it. He simply asks that you show up and do your part in the middle of the call.

Paul says in **Philippians 1:6 NLT, "And I am certain that God, who began the good work within you, will continue his work until it is finally finished on the day when Christ Jesus returns."** God finishes what He starts. He completes every work. I encourage you to finish every assignment you start. What good is a multitasker who works on thousands of projects simultaneously, but completes none of them? God created the world in six days. He didn't rest until He was finished. If God gives you something to do or someone to work with, complete the assignment. There is a reason He chose you.

The call on your life is important regardless to what you were called to do. Whatever God asks you to do is essential in the kingdom. We sometimes refuse to respond to the work of the call until we are certain of the call. It is easier to redirect something already in motion than to get something moving. It is important to keep moving and working toward your call. Sometimes stepping out on faith is the only way confirmation will come.

I was told when you don't know what to do, step out on faith and God will direct you. If you are headed in the wrong direction, He will lead you back to the path. Because He has your best interest at heart, He will redirect your steps if need be. Stepping out means you are at least willing to try to do what you think God wants.

Your destiny is decided by God. The call helps you to reach your predetermined destiny. Destiny involves more than just you. It involves getting done in the earth what God wants done to impact many. Throughout your life, if you pay attention as you walk out your call, you touch the lives of many. Every word God gives you that blesses you, blesses others as well.

My cousin was 19 years old when he died. I don't know what he was called to do, but on the day of his home going he had well over 400 hundred grieving people there from all walks of life. What if he was called to bring together a multitude of people to hear about the saving grace of God? What if his life and his death were about bridging a gap between families? What if he was called to bring joy to multiple families simultaneously? He did all those things.

He could have been chosen to show others they could have fun without succumbing to all the lures of the world. You do know that many are invited to participate in the plan God has, but not all accept and not all are chosen. **Matthew 22:14 KJV** says, **"For many are called, but few are chosen."** Not all teens are disobedient. In fact, some of them are very unique, and may appear peculiar to the world.

The called and the chosen must be called, chosen and faithful. I believe my cousin was faithful in the things God purposed for him to do. One thing that stood out was his love for family even at a young age. He came from a close knit family and he enjoyed spending time with his family. He was considerate for a young man.

He must have been a good friend, judging the amount of heart broken young people that came to say their goodbyes. Based on those qualities alone, it sounds like his mission was accomplished to me. As painful as it was to lose him so soon in life, I believe he fulfilled his call and reached his destiny. For so many people, it may take years to fulfill the call, but for others there is a bull's eye anointing that moves quickly. May he rest in peace knowing he is where he is supposed to be, in his destined place with God.

Reflecting on my cousin leads me to encourage you to respond to your invitation to do good. When someone is called to impact your life or to reach out to you, but never reaches out to you for whatever reason, I believe they hinder you from getting your stuff. Determine today to stop keeping people from getting their stuff from you. We are all pieces of the same puzzle. The same goes for someone called to bring another person out of bondage or to tear down the strongholds that bound them, and fail to do so.

Many people fail because of the tainted life he or she themselves live, which is detrimental to all involved. It's hard to pull someone else out of a pit when you yourself are in that very same pit and aren't doing anything to come out of it. In **2 Timothy 1:9 KJV**, the scripture talks about our call being a holy call. When we operate in holiness, it is easier to access others. Timothy says**, "Who hath saved us, and called us with an holy calling, not according to our works, but according to his own purpose and grace, which was given us in Christ Jesus before the world began."** God takes the call seriously and so should you. The call comes with wisdom, and provides growth opportunities so that you can mature in the call. Just because you are given a position description does not mean that you master it immediately.

Until you answer your call and begin working to respond to all that is associated with the call, you will not be at peace. You will have missing links in your life. Voids will spring from the left and right. Some things in ministry and in your life you will be aware of, while other things will be like trying to get through a maze.

Accepting your call is a sign of obedience. Walking out your call brings in the benefits. Living to please God with your call opens the door for added bonuses. You should desire to be obedient and to please God.

Some people take forever to say yes to the call. Some people half-heartedly participate in the call, picking and choosing the parts they want to do and negating the parts they don't want. When you finally jump in full fledge with your call, and God can trust you with it, He begins unfolding the bigger plan with your call in mind.

Not everyone rejects or runs from the call. I applaud those people. While the call intimidated me early on, I run toward it now. That's how I know the call is bigger than you or I realize. Initially, God doesn't share everything with you, but once He gets full cooperation, it will be like sitting on the porch sipping lemonade and chatting with God about what's next.

There is always a beginning, where you start, and a finish line, where God has seen you end. Maybe your call started with you joining intercessory prayer, but now He wants you to teach intercessory prayer. Maybe it started with you teaching a class, now He wants you to preach. Maybe it started with you preaching, now He wants you to pastor. Maybe it started with you pastoring; now He wants you to travel abroad sharing the Gospel. Maybe it started with you traveling abroad, now He wants you to counsel. Wherever your call starts, God can build upon it as you mature, or as there is need. The fullness of your call will be revealed to you as you grow in God.

It's like the song, "Yes" by Shekinah Glory. If I told you what I really want, would you still say yes? You have to say yes even before you see the details of what you're saying yes to. You can't read the terms and conditions, you just have to accept them. You can't read the contract first; you just have to sign the dotted line. Saying yes to the one who created you and the plan for your life is a win-win situation. Saying no is a bad, dead end decision.

Yes, you have free will and so did Jonah, but that didn't stop Jonah from landing in the belly of the great fish when he ran from God. You can run, but you cannot hide. There is no harm in surrendering; the harm is in running away. Jonah eventually did what God told him to do, but he hesitated in doing it.

Psalm 119:60 NIV says, **"I will hasten and not delay to obey your commands."** God doesn't have all day to wait for us to say yes. He doesn't even have to ask us. He could easily get whatever He wants done without us. But He involves us because He wants to give us opportunity to fellowship with Him.

Look at it from this perspective, when you say yes to the call, you accept a special invitation from God that allows you to join fellowship with Jesus. Paul says in **1 Corinthians 1:9 NLT, "God will do this, for he is faithful to do what he says, and he has invited you into partnership with his Son, Jesus Christ our Lord."** What better partnership to consider than this. He is a legitimate partner. He is the partner who will never sell out or cause you to have to compete against. He is the partner you should be partnering with.

Some trials come to show you how big your call is. I used to wonder why the opposition I faced came from leaders and people in high positions. Then one day, it was revealed to me. If I am constantly opposed by these people, it is because I rank among these people. I have surpassed the little ones and operate in the realm of those with authority and status. I too have authority and status, and the minute I recognized that authority and status and where it came from, my status changed.

Knowing the importance of your call and who you are is essential. When people think you don't know who you are, they are quick to challenge you. They will even throw daggers at you. Once they find out that you know who you are and they get a revelation of you, if they meant you harm, they retreat, running for cover.

You didn't choose the call. You didn't choose the authority that comes along with it either. But since you have been chosen to operate in the call, you may as well use your full authority. God's gifts and God's call are under full warranty, never cancelled, never rescinded. The call is irrevocable. **Romans 11:29 NLT says, "For God's gifts and his call can never be withdrawn."** God will elevate you within the call, but He doesn't withdraw the call. He may even add to the call, which means He is revealing to you the depths of the call that you weren't privy to at the start of the call.

How you define the call may be different from how God defines it. What the call entails may be revealed over a period of time, or it could be revealed instantly. God is sovereign and can do exactly as He wills to do. Whatever God decides, the question for you is, "What are you doing or going to do with your cross as you carry out the call?

Walking in Your Authentic Call . . .

> *1 John 2:27 ESV, "But the anointing that you received from him abides in you, and you have no need that anyone should teach you. But as his anointing teaches you about everything, and is true, and is no lie—just as it has taught you, abide in him."*

Some people think they can choose their call. Others think they can walk away from their call. Some just flat out say no to the call. Of course, there are those who are called one day and miss the call the next day. My dad says he believes some preachers go down through the woods and when they come back, they're a preacher. You do know that some preachers appoint themselves in the ministry.

Why on earth they would desire such a demanding assignment is beyond me. Surely it can't be the position, the status or the money, and if it is, there is so much more that comes along with the position, status and money. You give up so much to preach the gospel. It's a sacrifice that many don't fully contemplate. It's not a bad thing, but it requires much more than some calculate.

If you are not careful, as pastors, you spend so much time helping other families that you often neglect your own. You give so much to others that when you do make it home, you feel you cannot give another inch. You constantly put the needs of others above your needs. The majority of your life is spent operating in the help mode.

People are needy, and if they feel they can get what they need from you, they settle for you. I have had many people create research assignments for me to avoid seeking God or searching for themselves. There were those who depended on me as their Wikipedia because they weren't diligent in studying. Then, there's the boldness of others to assume it is your sole duty because you were called to preach and they were not.

Everyone has the same opportunity to have an intimate relationship with God. That also means they should desire to know Him for themselves which requires reading, studying and learning more about Him. While pastors and preachers bath in the word of God, you should not put your total reliance in them for your sole learning. When you do, if they take a break, does that mean you starve?

Shifting gears for a moment, there have been many who stood before the pastor and declared they were called to preach. After they were licensed to preach, they returned to that same pastor to say God was now calling them to sing on the choir, praise dance, join intercessory prayer, start a ministry or leave the church. Hmmm! Some went as far as to step down from the ministerial staff completely.

What I believe happened to a lot of them is they were afraid. From the outside it was glitter and glam, but after their call was confirmed and affirmed, the level of commitment and dedication was raised.

They were already doing the work, but once they were licensed, the work increased. They were already held accountable, yet when they received that certificate, they were called to a higher standard in more ways than one.

They were still washed in the Blood of the Lamb, and still redeemed by the Most High, but some of them couldn't handle the demands placed on them by the church. Some needed to make adjustments in their lives and finances. Some simply weren't ready to live all they preached. I think some came under such great attack that they figured if they left, the attacks would diminish. Mind you, some left because of people, which is unfortunate.

The good news is the ministers who were unsure as to whether they were actually called or not, had the sense to get out. God honors your commitment when you do something for good that you believe He told you to do. However, He makes clear what it is that He wants you to do. Sometimes, what He wants you to do resembles what you think He wants you to do.

Many don't consider, "To whom much is given, much is also required." **Luke 12:48 NIV** says, **"From everyone who has been given much, much will be demanded; and from the one who has been entrusted with much, much more will be asked."** Because of the assignment God has placed on your life, there will be times when it may seem overwhelming, but know it is not only expected of you, but it is also doable. When you consider the will of God, you must consider the demands, commitment, and requirements that come along with it.

The scripture says, **"But the one who did not know His master's will and did things worthy of punishment will receive a light beating. From everyone who has been given much, much will be required, and from the one who has been entrusted with much, even more will be asked."** So the statement, "To whom much is given, much is required," can be viewed in two ways. As ministers or disciples in general, we give a lot and will receive our just reward from the Lord as a result. Or you can view it this way, as ministers we are expected to give a lot because of the nature of the call, but we should also expect to receive a lot to be effective in that call.

As children of God, and what I like to call front-runners, you can expect the good, but you should also know that the not so good is part of the territory as well. Serving on the front line is part of the duties assigned. When you are essential, you have to show up when others take a break. If you are serving on the front line, you have to take hits that some will never feel. But through it all, you learn who you really are, and you learn how to operate out of who you are.

Learning to be your authentic self means being comfortable with who you are and what you are doing. When you are on a path to do what you were put on earth to do, most of what you do is part of your nature. You can only give what you have, or be who you are. It takes effort to try to be someone else, but you can be yourself without breaking a sweat. That's because God equips you with uniqueness, and with the qualities you need to do what He asks.

Being authentic causes you to operate in honesty and truth. There should be a genuine spirit attached to whatever you do. I have seen ushers and thought to myself, "God certainly did not call you to this position." There was an opening and they seized the moment. They had the right attitude for wanting to serve, but made the wrong decision in choosing the best position for them. If you know you are not a morning person, or aren't friendly, do not become a greeter. You know you don't feel like grinning and being perky first thing in the morning, so spare others.

I joined intercessory prayer because it was natural for me to talk to God on a daily basis. I could be me and talk to God at the same time. Early in ministry I was invited to pray at a prayer breakfast. Everyone who stood to pray yelled their prayers and perspired profusely, with spit flying. It was a sign to many that they could really pray. It wasn't my style, but when I stood to pray I followed suit. They cheered me on.

After I left the service, and knowing I was wrong, I shared the experience with my Dad. His words were, "You're not supposed to do what others do." I knew that, but I was trying to fit in. We weren't called to fit in, we are not robots. Otherwise, God would have made us all the same. How boring and ineffective would that be?

Now what I will say about that is, some people raise the bar when praying, thinking the louder and more intense they are when they pray, the more effective. I can imagine God wiping spit from the sides of the walls of the throne as they pray or having to wear hearing aids as a result of them yelling out their requests so loudly.

Yelling is the norm for some churches, and if you don't yell, some won't think you are as effective. The authentic you says, I will pray to my God the way I pray and you pray the way you pray. The desired goal is to talk to God and have Him talk to you. I have never heard God yell to me in prayer or in my daily walk. But I have heard a still quiet voice, a firm response, and a voice of authority. Even in my personal crisis when I was erratic, He remained calm. But if it's your nature to yell, carry on.

Being authentic requires you to be aligned with your core values. If you want the respect of others, you have to live a life worthy of respect. Paul says in **Ephesians 4:1 NLT, "Therefore, I a prisoner for serving the Lord, beg you to lead a life worthy of your calling, for you have been called by God."** Leaders need to be trustworthy if no one else appears to be. Think about the legacy you want to leave others. Think about who you represent as a leader. Ministry isn't about competition, it is about transforming lives. Paul begged in his letter to the Christians in Ephesus for them to live worthy, because he knew the benefits of being obedient to God.

Brace yourself. Now ponder this question. Are you sure of your calling? Do you really know what you are called to do? Have you gotten in over your head and feel you have to stay there? The answer to any question you may have can be found in the one who passes out assignments. Don't be afraid to go back and ask God if you heard correctly. It could be that you heard clearly, but He has made adjustments to the call. Or He is making adjustments in you.

Expanding the Assignment . . .

> ➤ *Romans 8:30 MSG, "God knew what he was doing from the very beginning. He decided from the outset to shape the lives of those who love him along the same lines as the life of his Son. The Son stands first in the line of humanity he restored. We see the original and intended shape of our lives there in him. After God made that decision of what his children should be like, he followed*

it up by calling people by name. After he called them by name, he set them on a solid basis with himself. And then, after getting them established, he stayed with them to the end, gloriously completing what he had begun."

Your call really is bigger than you realize. God prearranged your entire life from beginning to end. When He called you, it was because He had started a work and chose you to carry the work out. He saw the end result, and you were included in the calculation. When God was giving out calls, assignments and destined positions, He created you for a particular call, assignment and destined position. God custom made you for where you are going. He knows the entire path, where it starts and ends.

You cannot be afraid of where God is taking you or who He created you to be. God put His stamp of approval on you, and sealed you through redemption. Everything He put in you must come out of you. Every place He predestined for you, your feet shall be planted. The good news is while on the journey, God protects His righteous and He provides for them. Aren't you the righteous?

Ephesians 2:10 clearly states that you are God's handiwork. He has prearranged, pre-established, preplanned what you can and will do. You were recreated in Christ Jesus so that you can do the works God pre-destined for you to do. God prepared ahead of time things for you to walk in and carry out.

God has already prepared a path for you, and He will open the way for you to operate in your anointing. God already saw you doing what He has for you to do. The visions He gave you allow you to see what you will do. God saw you functioning and He made it possible for you to function just as He saw you.

I attended a conference where I met many professional African Americans, some prestigious and well esteemed. I spoke with one young lady in particular who confirmed much of what I already knew about myself, but added to my current knowledge as well. She gave me more details to the call I currently embrace. What she shared is much greater than where I am now.

I know our meeting was orchestrated by God. I can see God doing all the things she spoke of. Though I receive all she said, and

I am excited about some of what she said, I cannot take my focus off what I am trying to complete at this moment for God. I cannot afford to become anxious over what is about to happen and not finish the assignment at hand. I say that because in the past, whenever God spoke a word, I took off running whether I had details or not. I know sometimes God probably wanted to say, "Can you let me finish telling you before you run to do it."

I am aware that there will be seasons within the call. The call may even be gradual. Sometimes God will accept your response to the call and have you working on assignments long before He seals the deal in the natural. Then once it's settled, He may shift gears on the assignment He previously gave you. He may say, shift gears, we're going to do something different. If He says that to you, can you make the adjustment? It's still a part of the call, but you have to walk being open minded.

Obedience is part of the call. You might not agree with everything God is telling you, but you must obey everything God is telling you or suffer the consequences of disobedience. A costly example in the scripture is when Saul chose to carry out the portion of the instruction from God that he was comfortable with.

1 Samuel 15:22-23 NLT says, "But Samuel replied, "What is more pleasing to the Lord: your burnt offerings and sacrifices or your obedience to his voice? Listen! Obedience is better than sacrifice, and submission is better than offering the fat of rams. Rebellion is as sinful as witchcraft and stubbornness as bad as worshiping idols. So because you have rejected the command of the Lord, he has rejected you as king." Samuel figured out obedience was greater than any sacrifice or offering. Saul learned the difference too.

God may have you doing one thing for a season and something different for another season, but everything is still related to the call. Obedience means being able to adapt to the voice of God. When God chooses to add or subtract an assignment, your response has to be that of submission. Rebellion, stubbornness and rejection are all the same as sin, and disobedience.

Because your life has already been predetermined, God knows each assignment along the way. He understands why He is giving you something and why He might be taking something away from you. Can you handle the Sovereignty of God without Him having to sit you down and explain everything to you? His sovereignty also means He doesn't need your permission to lay out the foundation for your life.

The correct response to any assignment or instruction from God should reflect a willingness to surrender. "Whatever you want me to do Lord, I am your vessel! Whatever the assignment, my heart is open and I yield to you! I surrender my will to you! Use me for your Glory!" It is always about God's agenda, not yours.

Destiny is your appointed or ordained future. It is God's purpose for your life. Why not schedule your appointment with God today to discuss what He has predestined for you? It's okay to ask questions. After all, it is your life and it is you carrying out the call for God's purpose.

Some people check in week after week, asking other people to clarify their call. While many may be able to assist you in your call, I recommend that you sit at the feet of Jesus and ask Him about the call. That way you will know for yourself what you are accepting or potentially shying away from. He can clarify the call, while man may speculate about the call.

Don't get sidetracked by people's opinion. Some people mean well, while others don't. Fight your way through the negative voices of what those around you may think you should be doing and be sure you do what God says to do. Be determined to reach your destiny bringing God Glory.

As with Saul, you can seek to bring glory to people, or to God. I choose God. **1 Samuel 15:24 NLT** says, **Then Saul admitted to Samuel, "Yes, I have sinned. I have disobeyed your instructions and the Lord's command, for I was afraid of the people and did what they demanded."** At the end of the day, the opinion of people does not hold much weight. God's opinion about us is what's most important.

People may innocently misinform you or even attempt to hinder your call, but to no avail. The bottom line is God will not allow any person to keep you from your destiny. They may be bigger, stronger, or more powerful, but God knows how to shift things around and get you to where you're supposed to be.

I cannot recall a person throughout my journey who tried to hinder the call on my life. If it has been attempted, I was naïve then and I am naïve now. Sometimes we can be our own worst enemy, and because of our insecurities, we derail the process that leads in the direction of the call.

If you are going to be around for the next couple of years, why not make the best of those years. Live out your days in obedience to the voice of God and the Word of God. It has been said, and I believe it wholeheartedly, **"In the beginning was the Word, and the Word was with God, and the Word was God."(John 1:1 NIV)** God has been speaking His Word over our lives since the beginning.

He sent Jesus to earth to settle our future. **John 1:14 NIV** says, **"The Word became flesh and made his dwelling among us. We have seen his glory, the glory of the one and only Son, who came from the Father, full of grace and truth."** Within that future includes the grace and truth of our salvation.

Salvation is part of everyone's destiny, whether they choose to participate or not. Charles Stanley says, "God's plan for enlarging His kingdom is so simple – one person telling another about the Savior. Yet we're busy and full of excuses. Just remember, someone's eternal destiny is at stake. The joy you'll have when you meet that person in heaven will far exceed any discomfort you felt in sharing the gospel."

Every person will stand before God in response to salvation. Every person will stand before God whether they have a good report or negative report. They will give an account as it relates to their call and their ultimate destiny.

Everyone is not called to Pastor or preach from a pulpit. However, everyone has the responsibility of spreading the gospel of Jesus. Jesus said to the disciples in **Matthew 28:18-20 ESV, "All authority in heaven and on earth has been given to me. Go therefore and make disciples of all nations, baptizing them in the name of the Father and of the Son and of the Holy Spirit, teaching them to observe all that I have commanded you. And behold, I am with you always,**

to the end of the age." Everyone should have a track record of being an example in helping to make disciples of others.

In the Valley of Transition . . .

> ➢ *Ecclesiastes 7:8 ESV, "Better is the end of a thing than its beginning, and the patient in spirit is better than the proud in spirit."*

When you step out to do the will of God and it doesn't go quite as planned, or look like you thought it would look, does it mean God didn't tell you to step out? Certainly not! Obedience to the voice of God is never wrong or premature. God has a reason for everything— He does. You might not understand His reasoning, but do not be discouraged. It's not your job to understand why God does what He does; it's your job to do what He says.

Stepping out on faith is rather easy. Staying in the will of God is fairly easy. But walking in disobedience should not be an option for you at this stage of your life. During this season, God has literally handpicked you to do certain things.

God may release you to do a particular thing, and provide you with confirmation. However, confirmation does not mean you will immediately go directly to the place you think you should be at. And unfortunately, though you heard where you're going loud and clear, the first stop may not be it.

Transition is great because it is the process or period of changing from one state or condition to another. So God moves you from where you are, but He doesn't always take you straight to where you're going. Of course, there's a reason behind that move. He is positioning you, but where you're headed isn't ready for you, or you're not ready for where you're going.

Sometimes in the transition phase, you will discover you've actually been hidden. The thing about being in hiding is you won't necessarily get a memo stating that you're in hiding, though it would be nice. In fact, you will have been there for a while before you realize that's where you are. Hiding isn't a bad place, nor is it any less work. You are still expected to shine. You have to produce, be consistent and effective. The pace you're working at may appear to you as though you are out in the middle of Times Square working day and night, but you're not. You're in the valley of transition.

When you initially step out in response to the call and put into action the assignment, the message you will hear relayed to you is often, "This is what I want you to do." And because you are kingdom minded, you simply reply, "Okay Lord."

When you are in hiding, you are on basically on a need to know basis. Your assignments are restricted to what God wants to do in a particular area. If God doesn't purpose a thing to happen, it won't.

Transitioning from one thing to the next, either in action or state of being is necessary when aligned with the Will of God. Though you may not be where you want to be, your spirit has taken you through such growth spurs that it is impossible to remain as you were before the transition. Transition is a part of destiny.

It has been said, "The safest place to be is in the will of God." Any place in God is secure. If you have to be in hiding or in transition, as long as God meets you there, you're in good hands. God's protection is the most important state to be in. It's almost like being in a place where you know trial and error is to be taken seriously, but at the same time it won't disqualify you if you err.

Noah went through a protected season after he built the Ark. He obeyed God and took his family on the Ark. Though people didn't understand him, and obviously didn't believe him, he knew the importance of obeying God. It was proven that, regardless to what others did or believed, Noah was led by God. God preserved Noah at a time when He wanted to wipe out everyone and everything. He found favor with Noah before the Ark, kept him throughout the Ark, and then released him, causing great favor to manifest through him after the Ark.

Such is so with you, God will provide for you before He gives you the assignment. He will provide while you are carrying out His instruction, and well after you have been obedient to do all He has told you to do. In case you ever doubted, Noah is the witness that testifies to God's protection before, during and after the storm. You can expect the best when you have been faithful to walk upright.

Genesis 9:12-17 NIV says, And God said, "This is the sign of the covenant I am making between me and you and every living creature with you, a covenant for all generations to come: I have set my rainbow in the clouds, and it will be the sign of the covenant between me and the earth. Whenever I bring clouds over the earth and the rainbow appears in the clouds, I will remember my covenant between me and you and all living creatures of every kind.

Never again will the waters become a flood to destroy all life. Whenever the rainbow appears in the clouds, I will see it and remember the everlasting covenant between God and all living creatures of every kind on the earth." So God said to Noah, "This is the sign of the covenant I have established between me and all life on the earth." God remembers the covenant between you and Him. He will get you through each stage of your life on time.

It wasn't until years later that it was clear to me that I was in hiding. Imagine my surprise when I heard these words, "I released you, but I still have you in hiding." At first I didn't know how to take that. Then I was grateful for it. To me it meant I had not had the opportunity to be judged by the world, but I received the hands on experience of the assignment. So even if in looking back, if I messed up, I had a chance to get it right. It was sort of like a trial run.

Hiding or no hiding, I needed this experience to add to my Christian portfolio. It was necessary for where I am going. At the same time God was shielding me from much, and savoring me. While in this place, I never stopped working on the things I needed to do to help me in my future.

The Protected Season . . .

> *Leviticus 26:4 AMP, "I will give you rain in due season, and the land shall yield her increase and the trees of the field yield their fruit"*

Understanding the protected season is not something you automatically and immediately grasp as you are in that season. Sometimes it is not until you come out of the season that you find out it was a protected season. Maybe you didn't realize it because you were busy doing the work of the ministry. It is comparable to working in the ministry providing a particular service for years, and only after you have done so for so long, are you rewarded.

A man's gifts give him room and stand him before the great. **Proverbs 18:16 NIV** says, **"A gift opens the way and ushers the giver into the presence of the great."** Nothing I have done was a waste. And everything you have done is calculated and thankfully so. I tell my daughter with all the volunteer and unpaid internships she has done, jobs will chase her down and she will have to choose between positions.

In this season, as you continue to go forth in ministry reaching those God wants you to reach, allow your heart to be open to do whatever God leads you to do. The best place is a surrendered state, and opened to the will of God, whether you are in hiding or on display for countries to see. When you are this committed to God, and in a sold out capacity, your commitment is impressive to God. God rejoices because you started and are doing the work.

Ultimately, you are working because you love God and seek to please Him, but in doing so, your love has shown God that He can count on you. He knows, and you now know that you both are in agreement. He knows He wasn't wrong in choosing to trust you. No matter what you're working on, be determined to bring Glory to God every time you open your mouth.

Have you done something wrong to be in hiding? No, God's plan is at work. A mighty work is being accomplished even through places of seclusion. You have been launched out, yet many don't know you, haven't heard of you, and don't venture out to support you. Deep within you, know you are where you are supposed to be because of the confirmation you received for walking in obedience. The rewards are enough to make you stay the course and commit to God on a deeper level than ever before. Receiving the added bonuses just because you stepped out make you wish you had stepped out long ago.

When God does something for you that no man could do, there's nothing you will not do for Him in return. When God fixes a problem that plagued you for so many years, your heart has to go out to Him indefinitely. Just as the ten men with leprosy were cleansed **(Luke**

17:11-19 NIV) and one of them recognized his miraculous healing, and had the sense to go back and thank Jesus, I too went back to show my gratitude. Some things God will do for you, you will thank Him for the rest of your life with your life. Even while in the protected season, you see the favor of God in areas of your life that cause you to want to do more for God.

One thing about the protected season is that it can be the most rewarding, peaceful, and fulfilling place you have ever known. This confirms you heard your call correctly, and you are walking out the vision from the plan God set for you. Don't misunderstand the peace, fulfillment and reward as though the task is effortless. The only reason it appears manageable is because God renews your strength second by second. He gives you a fresh wind to accomplish all He set out to do in you and through you.

When I commuted to D.C. for work three years and three months, during that time I worked full-time, went to Seminary full-time, served in ministry full-time, authored books, embraced a husband and daughter, and managed the affairs of the household. During that season, God nurtured me through peace, nourished me through His Rhema word, and increased in me the ability to get multiple assignments done simultaneously. He kept me looking good on the outside and healthy inside while taking me through the process.

I was never without a song from God beginning at 3:00 a.m. every day. Those songs kept me in perfect peace daily. They were some of the motivation that kept my spirit lifted. David said in **Psalm 143:8 NASB, "Let me hear Your lovingkindness in the morning; For I trust in You; Teach me the way in which I should walk; For to You I lift up my soul."** God has been and remains faithful throughout the entire journey.

I was never without wisdom from God. He gave me daily prophetic messages for someone crossing my path without me asking. I lacked nothing while I did all I was required to do. Many would have fallen by the way side carrying out this assignment alone, but by the Grace of God I was well able because He was with me. The commute served as hands on perseverance training.

It was after those assignments ended or decreased that I grew tired. Not because God left me, but because the season was over for that assignment. Had I stayed, I would have been doing things in my own strength which could not have lasted long at all. God will ensure you have enough strength to do what He calls you to do. Endurance, Perseverance, Resilience, Diligence, Determination, Motivation, and Steadfastness are all attributes from God. Because God has those attributes, He can relinquish them to you. Talking about strength for the journey, this is something God graciously provides faithfully.

Your love for God and your reliance on God causes you to grow quickly, and learn fast as you carry out the assignment. You learn your strengths and you see your weaknesses. You find out why those attached to you are really there. You see the true motives of people as if it were written on a canvas. Many will pull from you, glean from you and monopolize your time, but will not give back. You must learn to take it with a grain of salt. You learn to give freely as God has given so freely to you.

In the protected season, there's no time to question where you are because God is continuing to do meaningful things in your midst. It's a precious time with God. You can see the benefits and you're grateful for them, but you also see that your progress doesn't look like those around you. Ringing loudly in the atmosphere are these words of encouragement, "Don't despise small beginnings." **Zechariah 4:10 NLT says, "Do not despise these small beginnings, for the Lord rejoices to see the work begin."** Besides, what you consider small may be monumental in God's eyes. One person's life changing event is worth God's time and effort.

God will set up camp in any neighborhood on any corner just to reach the one individual who will pass through. It's a compassionate heart that cares for one individual enough to prepare a moment in time for them to experience the love of God. When John the Baptist was in the wilderness yelling, "Repent" he didn't know who was going to come through, but he was in position to receive the one who came through.

Whether you are visibly seen or positioned in the mountainous areas like John the Baptist, your work is equally important. Jesus said in **Luke 7:28 NIV, "I tell you, among those born of women, there is no one greater than John."** Maybe you don't know how others view you, but do you know how Jesus views you?

John the Baptist was bold in his call and serious in his stance on preparing the way for Jesus. He went up against leaders, and proclaimed the gospel. He was driven and passionate about his call. He lived his life to introduce others to Christ. Do you believe God is calling you to introduce others to Christ? The same urgency that John the Baptist had is the same urgency you should have. **Jude 1:23 ESV says, "Save others by snatching them out of the fire; to others show mercy with fear, hating even the garment stained by the flesh."** You are supposed to go after those who take the wrong way. Jude says be tender with sinners, but not soft on sin. The sin itself stinks to high heaven.

While some see a place of hiding as a preparation zone, it is also viewed as a place where strict and direct orders are given by God. It's almost like a top secret assignment. There are those who God has targeted and you are the one God has released to go after them. That's a special assignment with a special anointing.

If you do not come out of hiding when you want to, it does not mean that God has placed a road block or detour in the plan that He has for you. Focus on the work and not the place He has you working in. God has not changed His plans for you. In fact, the plan you started out fulfilling is still being fulfilled, just not the way you thought it would be.

During seasons where God has you in hiding, people will attempt to give you a revelation of what is happening to you. Some of what they say may have validity and some of what they say may not. It has been said of certain positions and callings, you must be graced for. I do not disagree with that, but I would venture to say God graces you for whatever He calls you to. It has even been said that you cannot make God favor you. And of course I do not disagree with that statement either, but I believe you can cause God to want to favor you. And favor shows up at different times and in various ways.

Some people see you as failing the assignment if the results do not resemble the same or greater outcome as others. When measuring success, allow God to use His measuring stick. Reaching one is just as relevant and impressive as reaching one hundred. **Luke 15:10 KJV says, "Likewise, I say unto you, there is joy in the presence of the angels of God over one sinner that repenteth."** I think too many times we underestimate the impact that we have on others, or we allow others to minimize what we do for the kingdom if it's not all showy. We become competitive and put too much emphasis on comparison.

God's protection is definitely a place of safety. God knows the path you will travel, and He knows what it's going to take to get you there. If He decides to protect you from seen and unseen dangers, who are you to argue with or question that. You can't see what's down the road, what lies ahead, but He knows.

Thankfully, God sets up seasons in all of our lives, and He takes us through each season. It includes a seasonal time, a time of opportunity, and a fruitful time. It's easy to get frustrated when things don't occur on our time table, but the thing to remember is, every season is not harvest season, but every season is important.

There are plowing seasons which are needed. There are planting seasons which are needed. There are watering seasons which are needed. We prefer that every season be a time of increase, and ultimately they are. When you plow, you are on track. When you plant, you are on target. When you water, you are on point. There really is increase all around you. But without the other seasons, we wouldn't be prepared when the increase comes.

When the Temporary Provision Lifts . . .

> ➢ **Isaiah 43:16-19 NIV,** *"This is what the LORD says— he who made a way through the sea, a path through the mighty waters, who drew out the chariots and horses, the army and reinforcements together, and they lay there, never to rise again, extinguished, snuffed out like a wick: "Forget the former things; do not dwell on the past. See, I am doing a new thing! Now it springs up; do you not perceive it? I am making a way in the wilderness and streams in the wasteland."*

The thing about failure verses success is it may look different to others. Sometimes God will lift His temporary provision. When provision dries up, it forces us to change, and opportunity for that particular thing shuts down. You cannot hold on to something that God has considered done. The season has changed.

Don't try to make something last forever that wasn't meant to be permanent. The brook will dry up. You won't have someone bringing you manna or quail there because the provision has lifted. It doesn't mean you didn't hear correctly. It does mean that God isn't doing that any longer. He has moved on to something else and is doing something new.

Be grateful for the manna you did receive whether God sent it to you for a short period of time or a long period. Thank Him for providing the quail whether you received it six months or two years. Sometimes God may send the temporary provision to jump-start you, and to see how far you will take it. He may send it because it's what you need at that moment, and where you are. God knows it's not permanent, but you don't realize it.

I think in order for growth to take place, the temporary provision has to lift. It's equivalent to helping someone until they get on their feet. Twenty years later you should not be doing the same thing for the person. Helping someone for a season is great, but after that season your help has the potential to become habit forming. God doesn't want any of us to become dependent upon others. He wants us to grow from the experience.

Once the brook dries up, you cannot make what happened yesterday happen today. The plan of God will take you to new levels of faith. Though the place you begin at may seem like you are putting into action everything you learned prior to the assignment, it is still training ground. You may be plowing, but when God decides to shift, He just might remove you from the very location in which you are working on the assignment. That means the season is up at that location.

It's time for you to move into doing the next thing in the next season. Just because something was good when you started doesn't mean it is good now. Let go of the old so that you can receive the new. It's a stepping stone. Just because something ended, it doesn't necessarily make it a bad thing.

When a season is over, you can't keep putting time and energy into it. That's when it becomes more of a burden than a blessing. Nothing is forever except the word of God. Just because something doesn't last doesn't mean you missed it. Don't be too proud to say, "God I realize your favor has lifted and you're doing a new thing."

God has something greater for your future. But the season you were operating in is over; it did what it was supposed to do. It was another step towards your promised land. You have to take solace in the fact that what God has in your future is better than what you are letting go of.

John C. Maxwell says, "Failed plans should not be interpreted as a failed vision. Visions don't change, they are only refined. Plans rarely stay the same, and are scrapped or adjusted as needed. Be stubborn about the vision, but flexible with your plan." In other words, believe what you saw, but trust God with the details.

Don't doubt what you have done for God. Don't question where you're going in God. Don't regret where you've been with God. Don't underestimate your labor thus far. God has His hands on you.

Preparation . . .

> *Luke 12:35-40 ESV, "Stay dressed for action and keep your lamps burning, and be like men who are waiting for their master to come home from the wedding feast, so that they may open the door to him at once when he comes and knocks. Blessed are those servants whom the master finds awake when he comes. Truly, I say to you, he will dress himself for service and have them recline at table, and he will come and serve them. If he comes in the second watch, or in the third, and finds them awake, blessed are those servants! But know this, that if the master of the house had known at what hour the thief was coming, he would not have left his housed to be broken into. You also must be ready, for the Son of Man is coming at an hour you do not expect."*

I believe one of the reasons I take preparation seriously is because it's not a good feeling being caught off guard and ill prepared. To me, it's a missed opportunity. I had several dreams where I was in the perfect place of opportunity but I wasn't prepared. Once you're in that place you don't have time to go back and "get prepared," you have to "be prepared." I think it's more about being conscious of your environment, surrounding and staying alert. You never know when you are needed by God.

The Reverend Dr. Joseph Lyles once told me after I had responded to my call to preach and wanted to be licensed, "There is nothing wrong with preparation." When he made that statement, I accepted it because I respected Him as my Pastor. Now that I look back, God was preparing me for great things, and had exposed them to me, but it really wasn't the season to step into the fullness of what God was calling me to.

Yes I loved God, was obedient to God, sought to please Him, and was faithful to the ministry, but there are some things that I know now that I didn't know then. There are probably some things that I can handle now that I would have messed up then. I am glad I wasn't released back then. Everything your pastor does or doesn't do is not meant for evil. After all, if you believe it is God who brings increase in your life, then it is that same God who will manifest the increase.

Don't go stomping off pouting and miss your season because you cannot handle the preparatory season. Your call is bigger than you. You have others that are attached to you that you may not have met yet. It is important that you learn all the lessons you are supposed to learn. Go through all the phases you are destined to go through, and pick up all the wisdom you can attain. People are waiting on you, looking for you, and expecting your arrival. Your responsibility is to be sure you have what you are supposed to have for those people when you finally do reach your destined place.

If you are impatient, how you can teach someone else about patience? If you are known to stray from the path, how can you teach about obedience? If you haven't trusted God with your life, how can you offer the assurance to others? There's a lot to think about when you look at the full picture of instilling in others what has been instilled in you. Transference of what is on your life means you have something of worth to transfer. You have something that is needed that helps to sustain others. God is able to download whatever you need or may need more of while you are still in hiding.

Joseph could have seen the place he was in as a horrible pit, but God had already given him the dream long before the manifestation. As devastating as it was when his brothers threw him in the pit, and then sold him into slavery, not to mention being falsely accused of sleeping with Potiphar's wife, thrown into a dungeon over two years, and being taken from his father, Joseph later recognized it was the work of the Lord in order for his brothers to get the deliverance they needed down the road.

Genesis 45:4-11 NIV says, "Then Joseph said to his brothers, "Come close to me." When they had done so, he said, "I am your brother Joseph, the one you sold into Egypt! And now, do not be distressed and do not be angry with yourselves for selling me here, because it was to save lives that God sent me ahead of you. For two years now there has been famine in the land, and for the next five years there will be no plowing and reaping. But God sent me ahead of you to preserve for you a remnant on earth and to save your lives by a great deliverance. "So then, it was not you who sent me here, but God. He made me father to Pharaoh, lord of his entire household and ruler of all Egypt.

Now hurry back to my father and say to him, 'This is what your son Joseph says: God has made me lord of all Egypt. Come down to me; don't delay. You shall live in the region of Goshen and be near me—you, your children and grandchildren, your flocks and herds, and all you have. I will provide for you there, because five years of famine are still to come. Otherwise you and your household and all who belong to you will become destitute.'"

The dreams Joseph had were a part of his destiny. Unfortunately, his brothers could not handle his destiny until they benefited from it. The downside of revealing your destiny to others can be jealousy. You cannot always tell others what great things God has revealed to you. Some are insecure and may not be mature enough to handle what God has for you. Some will attempt to sabotage you. As sad as that is, it happens.

Use the place you are in to get done those things you were given to do. Don't procrastinate in the things you need to do. Use your time wisely. Whatever you are working on strive to get it done during this season. No time with God should be wasted time.

When God is with you, He is with you no matter what you go through. When God has His hands on you, there is no place He cannot reach you. There is nothing He won't do for you; nothing He will not protect you from. Despite your path, you are on the right path to your divine destined place, and you will get there on time.

It is easy to step out on faith doing the things God has called you to do. The question is, "Can you play the background when God wants to take lead in the things He has called you to do?" Christian hip hop artist Lecrae sings, "I can play the background. Sometimes, I know, I get in the way, so won't you take lead." Depending on how you answer that question will determine your ability to follow. Everyone wants to lead, but can everyone follow?

For me, it has always been about obeying the voice of God, whether leading or following. I learned how to stand down when instructed and proceed with caution when beckoned. One thing I won't do is follow through with something when I know God is saying not to. I gladly take a back seat for God, watching Him at work in my life and on my behalf.

Understanding the Call . . .

> *Ephesians 4:11-12 NASB, "And He gave some as apostles, and some as prophets, and some as evangelists, and some as pastors and teachers, for the equipping of the saints for the work of service, to the building up of the body of Christ."*

Moses' first response to the bigger picture of his call was, "Why me?" **Exodus 3:9-12 MSG, God said, "The Israelite cry for help has come to me, and I've seen for myself how cruelly they're being treated by the Egyptians. It's time for you to go back: I'm sending you to Pharaoh to bring my people, the People of Israel, out of Egypt."**

Moses answered God, "But why me? What makes you think that I could ever go to Pharaoh and lead the children of Israel out of Egypt?" "I'll be with you," God said. "And this will be the

proof that I am the one who sent you: **When you have brought my people out of Egypt, you will worship God right here at this very mountain."** Isn't that just like God to give you an assignment, comfort you in the midst, and send you on your way anyway with His assurance?

Moses raised several objections to God. He said, "They won't trust me. They won't listen to a word I say. "Master, please, I don't talk well. I've never been good with words, neither before nor after you spoke to me. I stutter and stammer."

GOD said, "And who do you think made the human mouth? And who makes some mute, some deaf, some sighted, some blind? Isn't it I, GOD? So, get going. I'll be right there with you—with your mouth! I'll be right there to teach you what to say." He said, **"Oh, Master, please! Send somebody else!" (Exodus 4:1; 10-13 MSG)** Moses didn't think he could handle the call. But God knew that he could. You might not be confident in your call but proceed under the instruction of the Lord anyhow and confidence will come.

Amos was minding his business doing what he was called to do when God expanded his assignment. **Amos 7:10-17 MSG** says, **"Amaziah, priest at the shrine at Bethel, sent a message to Jeroboam, king of Israel: "Amos is plotting to get rid of you; and he's doing it as an insider, working from within Israel. His talk will destroy the country. He's got to be silenced. Do you know what Amos is saying? 'Jeroboam will be killed. Israel is headed for exile.'**

Then Amaziah confronted Amos: "Seer, be on your way! Get out of here and go back to Judah where you came from! Hang out there. Do your preaching there. But no more preaching at Bethel! Don't show your face here again. This is the king's chapel. This is a royal shrine."

But Amos stood up to Amaziah: "I never set up to be a preacher, never had plans to be a preacher. I raised cattle and I pruned trees. Then GOD took me off the farm and said, 'Go preach to my people Israel.' "So listen to GOD's Word. You tell me, 'Don't preach to Israel. Don't say anything against the family of Isaac.'

But here's what God is telling you: Your wife will become a whore in town. Your children will get killed. Your land will be auctioned off. You will die homeless and friendless. And Israel will be hauled off to exile, far from home." Sometimes you will just have to say what God said and suffer the consequences. I would rather say what God said and take a backlash from people, than to not say what He says and take a backlash from God. I have been there and done that, saying exactly what God said.

People may come at you with claws, but if the message is from God, they cannot shoot the messenger. It really doesn't matter if you are banned from preaching as long as you say exactly what God says. You don't have to defend it; you just need to say it.

God called me to Pastor at a time when I didn't want to accept the call. I wasn't running from God, nor was I running from the work of God. I was running from what I didn't understand, what I didn't know and what I thought I knew. I had seen the ideal pastor. I somewhat knew the work that was involved personally and collectively. I didn't think it was in my makeup to carry out the assignment. Sure, I taught regularly, I preached sporadically, I spoke here and there. I prayed for folk, and led many to Christ on a weekly basis. But being a pastor is more than that.

Before accepting the call, it was as though I was cornered by God, and asked why the word Pastor frightened me so. Through tears, stuttering, and after listing all of my fears, concerns and reasons for running. God said to me, "You have it all wrong." That's because we want to be traditional and do things the way it's always been done. Some people think if you don't follow the normal format, God is not involved, which is so far from the truth.

Take the thief on the cross for example. He asked Jesus to remember him when He entered into His kingdom. Jesus assured him that he would be with Him in paradise **(Luke 23:39-43 AMP)**. But Jesus did not tell him to get down from the cross, go join a church, get baptized, speak in tongues then meet Him in heaven. He didn't make the thief do back flips, or quote ten scriptures first.

Often we feel we have to do what's been done and only that. I am discovering that God will sometimes use a traditional avenue to get you started, but He won't stick to it when He has greater things in mind. Traditional works in a lot of cases, and it is safe, but God works outside of the box at any given moment. If He didn't, the thief on the cross would have never seen heaven.

I was a minister who preached, taught and did the work of the ministry, and prior to saying yes to pastoring; I had visions, dreams and regular reality checks. I served faithfully, and I stepped out on faith. I was anointed, and I knew God heard my prayers and answered them. I knew how strong and powerful my connection to Him was, but I felt this assignment was a bit much.

For many reasons I said no, and for those same reasons I said yes. After saying yes to the call, for two and a half years I preached like never before, I taught more than I had ever taught. I prayed and interceded day and night, I sang hymns and solos until I thought I could cut a record. I did so many invocations and benedictions until they were oozing out of my pores. I had so many altar calls until I remembered the words in my sleep. I fasted, depending heavily on God. I drowned myself in the Word wanting more each time. I always felt the urge to go deeper and deeper.

I did what normal pastors do: communion, baby dedications, home going services, weddings, pre-marital counseling, deliverance, evangelism, outreach at the nursing homes and jails, feeding the homeless, helping families in need financially, spiritually and psychologically. I prayed for people I never met, I supported people I never saw, I ministered to people that only wanted a word when they were hurting, I laid hands on people who trusted the anointing on my life, to say what thus says the Lord, but never came back, like those nine lepers.

It was demanding indeed, but I devoted my life to doing what God told me He wanted me to do. It was rewarding to me in numerous ways, and my obedience blessed many. God did miraculous things for me and my family. But then it came to a screeching halt. You cannot put a price on the things He did for us, and everything He did wasn't for the world to see.

I learned a lot about people. I also learned a lot about myself. I am grateful for the learning experience and I am blessed to have that experience. Many stay in the same rut or place of complacency, never stepping out to do what God has called them to do.

When I left my old position, there were many people in various positions that remained. When I returned years later to my new position, most of those same people were still in their same old positions. That was baffling to me. It showed me they were intimidated to walk by faith. They lacked the courage that was needed to fulfill their assignment.

Isn't it funny how those same people that I just described are the first to question what you are doing? They prophesy to you, but won't work to fulfill the prophecy on their lives. Which is better? Stepping out in obedience in a protected season, or never stepping out at all, and sitting in disobedience. Those who do the least seem to be the very ones who attempt to judge, criticize and critique what others are doing.

When God decides to place a hedge of protection around you or hides you under the shadow of His wings will you complain? **Psalm 32:7 NIV** says, **"You are my hiding place; you will protect me from trouble and surround me with songs of deliverance."** You will be protected from those who are not assigned to you. Those who have impure motives will not be able to stay with you. Those who know you stand for holiness and refused to live holy won't be able to stomach you. But none of that matters as long as you continue to allow God to train you.

Psalm 32:8 NLT, The Lord says, "I will guide you along the best pathway for your life. I will advise you and watch over you." You have the assurance from God that though you don't understand it all, you don't have to worry about anything.

When you reach a point in your life where you can truly say if you died today or tomorrow that you are okay with your life, because you believe you are doing exactly what you are supposed to be doing, that's a place of serenity. Some don't know those serene places exist. Life does not have to beat you down every step of the way. It has priceless and cherished moments.

The call isn't just that of an Apostle, Prophet, Evangelist, Pastor, or Teacher. It also includes miracles workers, healers, helpers, organizers, and those who pray in tongues and the interpretation of tongues. **(1 Corinthians 12:8-10; 28 KJV)** It is also my belief that many are called to be peacemakers. **(Matthew 5:9)**

The Call brings Godly Contentment . . .

> ➢ *1 Corinthians 7:17 ESV, "Only let each person lead the life that the Lord has assigned to him, and to which God has called him."*

Some people enjoy their call, while others look like they swallowed sour lemons. You can have joy and peace in the midst of everyday events and life's activities. Good can come out of every negative situation, just as it comes out of positive things. **I Thessalonians 5:18 MSG** says, **"Be cheerful no matter what; pray all the time; thank God no matter what happens. This is the way God wants you who belong to Christ Jesus to live."** If you say you are in the will of God, or you want to be in the will of God, then do as Paul said, give thanks in all circumstances, for this is the will of God in Christ Jesus for you.

Though it was a lot of work, I was at peace week after week. I loved the time I spent with God preparing. He had previously told me the time I spent preparing was for me, not so much for Him. But I did it just the same because I desired to give my very best. I learned so much. And I was ever so grateful.

Sometimes God will lift you out of a season that you may want to hold onto. Ask yourself, do you want to stay there because you are content with your life and the path you are on? Do you think you have been stretched enough? Maybe that was one of the reasons for the screeching halt.

If you desire to stay somewhere after the season has shifted, your only reason should be that you are making certain that this is what God is telling you to do. Your most important concern should be pleasing God. If you are sitting out of season, let it be because you are awaiting confirmation and not denial.

Maybe what you did for God worked for that season but it's not working in the new season. A shift has to be made. In **2 Kings 7:3-5 ESV**, the scripture talks about four men who were lepers at the entrance to the gate where the Syrians were supposed to be camped. And they said to one another, **"Why are we sitting here until we die? If we say, 'Let us enter the city' the famine is in the city, and we shall die there. And if we sit here, we die also. So now come,**

let us go over to the camp of the Syrians. If they spare our lives we shall live, and if they kill us we shall but die." One thing was certain for the four men of leprosy; if they stayed there, they would surely have died. They didn't know for certain if they would die if they went, until they went.

There will come a time in your life when you are faced with staying or going. When you know if you stay you will die, but you think if you go you might die, read about the four men of leprosy. I'm sure if they were here today they would probably advise that you GO! Just as God stepped in and made a way for the four men, and they lived to tell about it, He will do the same for you. Don't be afraid of the unknown, or of uncertainty. God promises to be with you. Don't worry about what's ahead, especially when God is taking you there.

Contentment does not mean that everything is perfect. Nor does it mean that you have everything you want or need in ministry. Contentment is when you know that the hand of God rests upon your life. When you operate from a place orchestrated by God, you move through levels of confidence. Your expectancy increases, causing expansion in your life.

God will send an unusual bunch of people to you during this season, and though you may not understand why they are there initially, you will quickly find out. God knows what each of His children stand in need of before they know. He will allow you to plant seeds in some, water the seeds that were already planted in others, and He will bring forth the increase.

Planting seeds can consist of ministering the word through teaching or preaching to an individual. It can come through testimony or forms of encouragement. It can come through mentoring, or investing time with an individual. Though there are various ways, it is in essence pouring out the knowledge and experiences you have with a particular subject. The bottom line is you are giving a person something now that they may not think they need, and it is being stored up for later use. Or you are giving them something now that they will definitely need later.

Watering seeds consists of reiterating to someone what they have already heard and causing them to get the revelation of what they heard in hopes of putting it into practice. You may have heard about salvation, but if you don't know what you must do to receive salvation, you won't be saved. Watering involves teaching application, giving demonstrations, and providing examples through the Word which consist of teaching, preaching, testimonies, encouragement, mentoring or investment. It is not limited to these but can include these.

The increase comes when God takes what you heard, what you learned, what you know and expounds upon it. He brings you to a place of accountability. He gives a revelation of what you heard, what was planted, and He takes what you learned, what was watered and pours on increase which allows you to walk in wisdom and maturity. God may use others to woo you into the kingdom, but He draws you to Him and invites you in to make His abode with you.

The one who plants is not the one to be highlighted, neither is the one who waters the one to be highlighted. Neither the planter nor the waterer can do anything without Christ's aid. The crucial one is He who gives the increase. God gives them their abilities, and assist them in the exercise of their gifts. **1 Corinthians 3:7 NLT** says, **"It's not important who does the planting, or who does the watering. What's important is that God makes the seed grow."**

Each thing you do is a stepping stone to what you are going to do. I accepted Jesus as Lord and Savior, became a disciple, and studied to learn more about God. I joined church, got baptized, and began fellowshipping with other believers. I attended Sunday school, Bible Study and Worship services. I participated in church activities, got involved in church ministries and lived the best life I knew to live. Doing those things led to me wanting to know more and be better.

I went to Bible College to learn more about God and as a way of keeping me disciplined to stay in the Word. Those classes led to me wanting to respond to ministry. I began teaching bible studies, participating in evangelism, leading children's Church and praying way more than I ever had. I wanted to go deeper in God as I was not satisfied. I learned to go from praise to worship, which was the most effective move I had made up to this point.

Still not satisfied, I desired more and entered into travail and whaling in deep worship. This allowed me to cross over into speaking in tongues and strengthening my prayers. Prayers became more intimate. I learned how to fight and to war in the spirit. I began recognizing the authority and greatness on the inside of me and wanted to pursue God even further.

I started a nonprofit 501 3c organization and worked in the vineyard for many years. It was fulfilling, but soon I had that longing to do more. I knew there had to be more. I served on intercessory prayer, interceding for thousands; I served on evangelism, leading thousands to Christ. Yet I wanted to go deeper in the things of God. This was work that I enjoyed and committed to wholeheartedly, but still there was more I desired. This new found revelation led me to go to seminary where I learned who I was, what I was called to do and what God wanted to do through me.

Upon completing seminary, it was time to put all the knowledge, wisdom and experience into action. I continued teaching, preaching, mentoring, counseling, and reaching out to others as God led. There came a new level of spirit led instruction that launched me out further into what God wanted for me. I began pastoring a flock as diligently as I knew how. Because I am a giver and always a student, I ventured into the Doctoral program, with the desire to be the best possible help to others I could possibly be.

As I stated before, as a pastor I felt like I talked people off ledges daily. The good news was God provided the cure for keeping them off that ledge. Entering into the pastorate and doctoral program simultaneously opened my heart to counseling. Counseling was an element many lacked in their Christian journey. While focusing on counseling and feeling the urgency to make myself available to those with an emotional or psychological need, my thinking was elevated and heart expanded from those hurting to those causing the hurt.

The call is much grander than you understand. It does not stop there, but up to this point I have demonstrated the complexity of the call. If God had to sit down and explain to you from day one all that you would be expected to do within the call, you would probably pass out or become prideful. So He piece meals us until we are mature enough to handle the call.

There were many people who played a role in planting seeds in my life. Many came along and watered the seeds that were planted.

But as you can see, God gave the increase and caused what once was a seed to produce and allow me to become a harvester.

My name means Reaper, Harvester. When I was born, I didn't know what my name meant. As I got older I found out what it meant but I didn't know what it meant as far as what I would be doing. Now I see portions of what that could possibly mean, but I don't have the full picture. I have more information than I am mentioning here, but I know there's more than I know or have been told by God. I know eyes have not seen, nor ears heard, neither have entered into the heart of man what God has in store for them who love Him **(1 Corinthians 2:9 KJV)**. The mind can't even imagine all the things God has and is waiting to disburse to His beloved children.

And so I go to the scripture in **Luke 24:45 NIV** that says, **"Then he opened their minds so they could understand the Scriptures."** God provides insight to you, and He opens your heart so that you can respond. When you understand scripture you comprehend the heart of God. That comprehension leads to genuine action in the things of God, and right standing with God.

As you reflect on your call, though you may not see the full picture in the beginning, you can rest assured that the portion God does give you is satisfying. **Proverbs 3:13-18 KJV** says, **"Happy is the man that findeth wisdom, and the man that getteth understanding. For the merchandise of it is better than the merchandise of silver, and the gain thereof than fine gold.**

She is more precious than rubies; and all the things thou canst desire are not to be compared unto her. Length of days is in her right hand; and in her left hand riches and honour. Her ways are ways of pleasantness, and all her paths are peace. She is a tree of life to them that lay hold upon her: and happy is every one that retaineth her." Be happy with the knowledge and understanding that you do get, but don't get bent out of shape when you don't get all the answers you think you need. Some things are on a need to know basis.

An old but faithful **proverb** in **chapter three verse five** says, **"Trust in the Lord with all your heart, and lean not on your own understanding."** Sometimes you just have to trust what you don't understand. **Jeremiah 17:7 NLT** says, **"But blessed are those** who trust in the Lord and have made the Lord their hope and confidence." My trust is in God. He is my confidence.

My Response to the Call . . .

> *Colossians 1:15-23 NIV, "The Son is the image of the invisible God, the firstborn over all creation. For in him all things were created: things in heaven and on earth, visible and invisible, whether thrones or powers or rulers or authorities; all things have been created through him and for him. He is before all things, and in him all things hold together. And he is the head of the body, the church; he is the beginning and the firstborn from among the dead, so that in everything he might have the supremacy. For God was pleased to have all his fullness dwell in him, and through him to reconcile to himself all things, whether things on earth or things in heaven, by making peace through his blood, shed on the cross. Once you were alienated from God and were enemies in your minds because of[1] your evil behavior. But now he has reconciled you by Christ's physical body through death to present you holy in his sight, without blemish and free from accusation— if you continue in your faith, established and firm, and do not move from the hope held out in the gospel. This is the gospel that you heard and that has been proclaimed to every creature under heaven, and of which I, Paul, have become a servant."*

The most peaceful I have ever been in my life was when I began pastoring. That kind of peace is priceless. I would not trade wealth for such place of peace. To hear God so clearly and to feel His presence so strong is unmeasurable. To sit at His feet and be fed, filled, and comforted is beyond silver and gold.

Today I am at a place of peace. I have many assignments to fulfill, but I feel good about my life. I smile on the inside and it shows on the outside. I know God loves me, favors me and wants me to win. I have the good life that God set up ahead of time for me. I stand in the presence of the Almighty God who has everything that I need.

I endeavor to enjoy the gifts that I have, the talents I have been given and the path God has placed me on. I am excited about what I know God has planned for me. I receive the assignment on my life. I know I am going to succeed because I am in the will of God. I wait with tiptoe anticipation to operate at the highest level God has prearranged for me.

I know I am one of God's chosen vessels. I know He cares about everything that concerns me. The places He has shown me, things He has done, and revelations He has given me are rewards that I will forever cherish. Yet I know the places He will take me, things He will do, and future revelations will push me into the overflow in every area of my life.

I like how Paul lays it out in the message translation in **Colossians 1:15-23**. Paul says, **"We look at this Son and see the God who cannot be seen. We look at this Son and see God's original purpose in everything created. For everything, absolutely everything, above and below, visible and invisible, rank after rank after rank of angels—*everything* got started in him and finds its purpose in him. He was there before any of it came into existence and holds it all together right up to this moment. And when it comes to the church, he organizes and holds it together, like a head does a body.**

He was supreme in the beginning and—leading the resurrection parade—he is supreme in the end. From beginning to end he's there, towering far above everything, everyone. So spacious is he, so roomy, that everything of God finds its proper place in him without crowding. Not only that, but all the broken and dislocated pieces of the universe—people and things, animals and atoms—get properly fixed and fit together in vibrant harmonies, all because of his death, his blood that poured down from the cross.

You yourselves are a case study of what he does. At one time you all had your backs turned to God, thinking rebellious thoughts of him, giving him trouble every chance you got. But now, by giving himself completely at the Cross, actually *dying* for you, Christ brought you over to God's side and put your lives together, whole and holy in his presence. You don't walk away

from a gift like that! You stay grounded and steady in that bond of trust, constantly tuned in to the Message, careful not to be distracted or diverted. There is no other Message—just this one. Every creature under heaven gets this same Message. I, Paul, am a messenger of this Message.

I, Teresa, am a messenger of this Message. I accept the call whatever it entails. I walk boldly to my destiny.

Chapter Four

The Heart: A Hard Place

"I know it hurts, but it is necessary"

Even in the will of God you will experience things that you cannot immediately make sense of. You are expected to produce under pressure, despite the pressures. Just because you are in the will of God doesn't mean those around you are. It is important that you understand your value and respect it. You have the power to contend. Whatever hurdle comes your way, you can jump over. Whatever giant comes your way, you have the power to slay.

Some seasons are designed to show you what you're made of. Some seasons will test your endurance and if you cannot make it in these particular seasons, you won't be promoted. The reality of your situation will literally stand face to face with you and challenge you to sink or swim. You don't have to sink, whether you know how to swim or not.

At a time when I needed assurance, God provided it. One day as I attempted to turn my cell phone off, a scripture kept appearing that prevented me from shutting down the phone. I knew without a doubt this scripture forcing its way to reach my attention was total assurance from God. Up to that moment, I had never even read that scriptural verse before.

The scripture that appeared so urgently on my phone was a result of a spiritual attack that launched a physical attack against me. When you are in the will of God, it does not matter what attacks are designed to come against you, God can block any attack. He will get His message to you regardless to where you are. God will also provide for you in advance to help minimize the attack. For me, God's word came at a time when I was clearly under attack. But despite the attack, God wanted me to rest in Him, realizing He had it all under control.

When you are in a threatening situation, you cannot control what others do or how they act, but you can control what you do and how you react. This is the prophetic message God gave Zephaniah that provided me with assurance regarding safety when I needed it most. **Zephaniah 3:17 NIV** says, **"The Lord your God is with you, the mighty Warrior Who saves, He will take great delight in you, in his love he will no longer rebuke you, but will rejoice over you with singing."**

God protects us in ways we don't even know. The enemy will attempt to launch attacks, but your dependence on God can greatly influence situations and bring about immediate peace. While I didn't understand the full attack, nor did I know what was launched against me totally, I understood the full covering God had placed over my life. I understood how much God loved and favored me. I understood my value and I knew God took great delight in me.

Controlling Your Emotions . . .

> ➤ *Joshua 1:9 ESV, "Have I not commanded you? Be strong and courageous. Do not be frightened and do not be dismayed, for the LORD your God is with you wherever you go."*

It is safe to say that everyone deals with some type of emotion. Acknowledging the emotion is good despite what emotion it is. It's easy to push emotions aside temporarily, but just because you are not reacting to an emotion doesn't mean it doesn't exist. Controlling your emotions doesn't mean ignoring or repressing them. Controlling your emotions means learning to process them, and respond to them in a healthy manner. You can learn to regulate your emotions.

Sometimes our physical or emotional side will react to situations in a way that the spiritual side would not. God's word came at a time when I needed to keep my emotions in tack. I could only keep them in tack by trusting the word of God that came immediately before I could utter the words, "Help me Lord!"

Multiple attacks were launched against me simultaneously, Church, School, Work, Health, Marriage, and Home. These attacks hit every area of concern to me at the same time. It's one thing to get hit, but when you're getting hit from every angle, it's hard to duck or cover up. All these attacks came like a mighty rushing wind; not to mention dealing with multiple tragic deaths of loved ones. But thank God He steps in and moves you out of the way before you get taken out.

With all of these attacks, I was holding on for dear life. I didn't have time to stop and call ten people. I was thrust in a fight and had to fight my way out. I referenced this scripture earlier, but it's worth repeating. Looking back, sure I was afflicted in every way, but not crushed; perplexed, but not driven to despair; persecuted, but not forsaken; struck down, but not destroyed.

Paul describes it well in **2 Corinthians 4:8-12 GNT, "We are often troubled, but not crushed; sometimes in doubt but never in despair; there are many enemies, but we are never without a friend; and though badly hurt at times, we are not destroyed."** Thankfully God revealed to me early on that much of what was launched against me, He stopped. He didn't tell me what He stopped, but I'm good with knowing that He stopped some attacks that were launched against me.

You cannot discount God in any season, and that also means you cannot keep a child of God down. I know I am on the most wanted list by the enemy, but I also know he cannot do anymore to me than my Father allows. Just as the enemy wants me for evil, God wants me for good. I am on the most loved list with God. I'm on the most favored list of God.

My husband often tells me he knows I am surely one of God's favorite. He has seen God come to my aid in many instances. He has evidence of God at work in an effort to bless and protect me. It is important to know how God sees you and goes to battle for you and over you.

When you go through trials in life, grab onto the Word of God and allow it to preserve your life. Believe it or not, trials were incorporated in the plan for your life, but it was originally placed there for good. No trial was sent to destroy you, or to overcome you. Remember, Jesus went through trials we cannot comprehend. But He came prepared before the trial to show us how to overcome, declaring us more than conquerors.

Some things I have gone through hurt so bad, or caused so much anxiety, stress, pain, pressures, hurt, and disappointment that it felt like at times it was designed to make me quit. But despite those feelings which were very real, I knew within my knowing that quitting was not an option. I knew within my spirit and at my very core that God would not allow any of my storms to destroy me.

God doesn't waste anything. He uses everything for good. The attacks launched against me ended up teaching me, growing me, equipping me, and giving me the experience that I needed. Though it was designed to show me people, it also showed me "me." I knew, though the enemy meant evil, and those storms were set up or orchestrated to tear me down, God used all of my pain and weaknesses to build me up and give me strength.

Many times, I considered throwing in the towel or simply not fighting back. But just as fast as the thought entered in, God gave me restored breath. I didn't have to gasp for air as if my supply were cut off. I just needed to regroup. It is so important to take time to refocus your thoughts and breathe even in battle.

There is a defining moment when you talk about throwing in the towel, or to fight or not to fight. If you're going to hang on to God you have to hang on to God. If you're going to hang on to your emotions and feelings, you hang on to that. I chose to hang in there and hold on despite how I felt, and despite how I hurt. Sometimes it felt like I was losing my footing. But I have learned if you hold on to God when you're hurting, weak, struggling or tired, things will turn around.

Things will work in your favor as it did for me. Things will be so much better and on such a grander scale. But you have to fight with everything in you. You have to push when you don't feel like pushing. You have to be determined to not grow weary in well doing. Knowing that the weapons will always form against you but they will not prosper. Keep pushing, plowing, working, moving and striving until you reach where God wants you.

It's a hard place that you must go through. It is an extremely hard place, but I'm telling you from experience with every ache, every pain, every trial, and through every ounce of persecution, God was with me. He never left me and He never failed me. And just as He was with me, He will always be with you. I couldn't have made it through anything that I made it through without the Grace of God. People lied on me, questioned me, and abandoned me, but through it all God was there. He loved me, and comforted me. Even if He didn't speak, I knew He was there.

There was never a time in my life when I didn't know that God was with me. There were some painful and devastating moments, but because of those times, I know God far greater than I ever would have. And I wouldn't change those times, as lonely as they were, and as dark as some times were.

God is all we have. He put people in our lives, but God is ultimately all we have. He is the only one who truly understands us or what we go through. He is the only one that deciphers our groans. He is the only one that does not reject us. He is the only one who loves us unconditionally. I would not trade anything for Him, not fame, money or people. Without Him I would totally be insane. My life would be a total mess. I would be miserable, lifeless, and unfulfilled.

As a result of those multiple attacks, I cried two months straight. It angered me to cry for so long, not being able to stop the tears even if I wanted to. I saw it as weakness at first, but I knew it was also working as a purging agent. I accepted the tears and allowed them to run their course freely. But my response is, with all I endured, "If that's the best the enemy could do to me was to cause my emotions to be out of whack, with streaming tears down my face, then he lost again."

God sure put my emotions back together. He evicted fear. He kept anger at bay. He deported sadness. Depression could not take root. He kept reacquainting me with joy, and joy slept at the foot of my bed daily. Whenever I had the urge to feel disgust, trust reminded me it was sitting beside me minute by minute.

I anticipated the end result. I knew from the beginning it would be that of victory and never defeat. I expected to win and even pitied the fate of the enemy. I was surprised by the attacks but it just proved the power and authority I walked in.

Trust the God in You . . .

> *1 John 4:4 NLT, "But you belong to God, my dear children. You have already won a victory over those*

> ***people, because the Spirit who lives in you is greater than the spirit who lives in the world."***

I love God with everything in me and I will serve Him until the day I die. I don't care how many times my heart is broken, how many times I am disappointed. He will always be my salvation. I will always be rooted and grounded in Him.

When faced with decisions that you do not have answers for, it can easily bring out the irritable side of you. It can cause you to operate in levels of stress, which adds frustration. Whether you are clear in the direction to take or not, you have to rely more than ever on God.

Stepping out in faith is commendable. Surrendering to the will of God is rewarding. Trusting God is promising. Doing the work of God is fulfilling. Yet there will be times when things may not quite line up the way you think they should or imagined they would. In these times solicited and unsolicited prophecies may come left and right, and you may receive them all, but what happens when they do not come to pass?

What do you do when what you are doing is simply not working effectively? Do not allow discouragement to set in. When you are faced with major decisions that impact the lives of others, the best advice is to fast and pray until you get your answer. Once that answer comes, be at peace with it. The most important concern you should have is pleasing God. If God is pleased with your decision and if He is involved in the decision making process, it shall be well with your soul.

Ponder this question, "Is your heart in what you're doing? Or are you concerned with what people think about what you're doing?" There will come a time when you come to the crossroad and must decide whether you will do a thing to look good before people, or discontinue a thing to look good before God. People may never see that God is satisfied with your decision. But then again, people are not who you have to answer to at the end of the day. As long as when you lay your head to rest, you sleep well at night; people's opinions don't hold much weight.

A word of caution, "If you are not careful, having too many whispering in your ear can lead to you feelings of ineffectiveness." When you are trying to find your way, spend time with God. His words are life-giving, and life-nourishing. Listen to the One who offers sure, solid wisdom and enduring love.

Isaiah 55:1-5 KJV says, **"Ho, every one that thirsteth, come ye to the waters, and he that hath no money; come ye, buy, and eat; yea, come, buy wine and milk without money and without price. Wherefore do ye spend money for that which is not bread? and your labour for that which satisfieth not? hearken diligently unto me, and eat ye that which is good, and let your soul delight inself in fatness. Incline your ear, and come unto me: hear, and your soul shall live and I will make an everlasting covenant with you, even the sure mercies of David."** Go to the source and get exactly what you need.

People are generally giving you what they got from God if they are genuine. That means you too can go to God. You cannot be lazy when it concerns your life and your future. You cannot become overly dependent on others to solve your problems, especially when you yourself have been granted open access to the throne of Grace.

One of the lessons I learned early on in ministry at a time when I ran from prophet to prophet, preacher to preacher, and conference to conference "Trust the God in you." Get answers from God personally. If push comes to shove, get confirmation from those God has put in place, but do not allow them to become the source you start with and the source you end with. **James 1:5 NASB** says, **"But if any of you lacks wisdom, let him ask of God, who gives to all generously and without reproach, and it will be given to him."** God is the author and finisher of our faith.

Deeper Levels of Trust . . .

> ➢ **Proverbs 3:5-6 NLT,** *"Trust in the LORD with all your heart; do not depend on your own understanding. Seek his will in all you do, and he will show you which path to take."*

Did you know you can be in the will of God, doing exactly what you are supposed to be doing when all of a sudden you get derailed? It happened to me. One would think if you are doing a Christian thing, in a Christian atmosphere, with Christian people that you are safe. Well let me tell you, Jesus was doing the Christian thing, in a Christian atmosphere, with Christian people, and had to stand in the face of adversity despite the good.

My graduate experience took me to deeper levels of trust and knowing in God. The attacks came in the form of deception. It was an attempt to cause me to feel inadequate. I had sore wrists from typing days on end with only bathroom breaks. Blood shot stained red eyes that blurred and teared from sleep deprivation. My jaw dropped leaving my mouth hanging open from exhaustion. My body was numb from sitting twenty hours straight at a time. I got two hours of sleep sporadically over a three week period.

I produced more work in two weeks than some would do in a semester. It was so challenging that my diet was compromised. I ate 94% fat free popcorn, veggie platters, pinto beans, drank hot tea, V8 juice, and whatever God led me to eat during what felt like survival boot camp.

These spiritual attacks came at the highest alert and were designed to make me quit. I received phone calls daily telling me I could not finish; I would not be able to finish the required work. The voice on the other end of the phone constantly said, "You're not going to walk across the stage. You might graduate later, but you won't walk in the coming months as scheduled."

I felt like a boxer in a ring. I kept getting hit and as I was going down, the crowd yelled, "Stay down!" But I kept getting back up. I could not quit. There were moments when I was so overwhelmed that I wanted to quit, but I could not. My mentality combined with my determination, ego and pride made me fight regardless to how many times I was hit, and regardless to being hit below the belt. All I heard in my spirit was keep plowing. Don't allow the voices to enter in, just keep plowing until it's over. Ignore all the comments, discouragement, negative remarks, choose to keep plowing.

I couldn't stop even if I wanted to. I got to a place where I didn't know how to stop. I couldn't turn that drive and momentum off. It was as if I was forcing myself inwardly to keep trusting and working. I trusted God and I knew God had the final say. But I didn't have time to stop and figure out what to do. I had to "do." I knew continuing to work was all the fight I had left in me. All I could do was work until I reached a completed stage and wait for the response.

I had the vision of crossing the finish line. I had the dream that I made it across the finish line. Outside of that, I didn't know how I would get through. I tried to focus on plowing and not what it was costing me.

I was forced to jump through hoops continuously. One thing that was designed to be a setback was the fact that I had to incorporate forty additional books to my research in a week. Not only that, but from the subject in which I wrote on, the books could be no later than year 2010. The enemy miscalculated reading and incorporating information was my strength. As if that wasn't enough, another tactic of the enemy was to have me change the format of over three hundred footnotes in a week.

I was told to remove resourceful research that was relevant to my topic though it was approved and included a year prior. I had to change the format back and forth from week to week, satisfying the opinion of others as often as they wanted. This inconsistency caused me to have to pay two editors to comb through much contradiction.

Though I was under attack viciously, the worst part was discovering all of my hard work that was critiqued and challenged every step of the way, was being taken from me and used as personal gain before I even received a passing grade. I had not given permission for my work to be used. It was very discouraging as I had future plans to use it the same way.

I could not choose those I worked with—they were assigned to me. Half way through the assignment, the person I had been assigned to for three years suddenly had to cut his workload by shifting seventy-five percent of the students under someone else's direction. It proved to be a blessing in disguise, but the process was designed to cause me not to complete the requirements on time.

I paid months and months well over the time needed for survey instruments to ensure the information was available should I have to produce it at a later time. This process was so stressful that I felt like I was functioning on fumes. My husband said as he watched me work, there was an aura around me. He said if my head fell downward from exhaustion, seconds later it would be pushed back up, and I continued working.

Despite the challenges, I made it. When I reached the finish line, I walked with my chest stuck out with pride. As I walked out among the crowd of thousands upon thousands of people, my knees buckled and I cried as though everything in my body had finally given me permission to release all the tension and stress.

My gratitude appeared to burst at the seams as the storm was officially over. I won the battle, and passed the test. Some people don't recognize the distinction between gratitude and despair. I shared with a woman how God brought me through and my reaction to Him bringing me through. I told her as I reflected on the finish line, I was overwhelmed with tears. She questioned if I was pre-menopausal. Where on earth did that come from? Grateful is what I was and remain.

I had to take time to recover from the graduate experience, but I walked in total victory. Never underestimate the power on the inside of you. Never give up on what you know God has led you to. Believers can sometime put you through more than unbelievers. But at least you expect it from unbelievers. The world does what it does to hinder you, but Christians ought to be different.

Paul says in **Ephesians 6:11-12 ESV, "Put on the whole armor of God, that you may be able to stand against the schemes of the devil. For we do not wrestle against flesh and blood, but against the rulers, against the authorities, against the cosmic powers over this present darkness, against the spiritual forces of evil in the heavenly places.** Remember who you are fighting. It's the enemy, not people.

My experience was, people appeared as though they started out with me, but turned into my worst nightmare toward the end. Then once I conquered, they were with me again. As much as they were eager to dismiss me, I was just as eager to prove to them that the God on the inside of me was stronger. Paul continues in **Ephesians 6:13-16, "Therefore take up the whole armor of God, that you** may be able to withstand in the evil day, and having done all, to stand firm. Stand therefore, having fastened on the belt of truth, and having put on the breastplate of righteousness, and, as shoes for your feet, having put on the readiness given by the gospel of peace."

Some things fight fiercely against you because of the importance of what you're doing and the impact your work will have on lives to come. That's why you have to fight harder. Paul says in **Ephesians 6:17, "In all circumstances take up the shield of faith, with which you can extinguish all the flaming darts of the evil one; and take the helmet of salvation, and the sword of the Spirit, which is the word of God."** You cannot lose with the word of God.

Strengths verses Weaknesses . . .

> *Isaiah 40:28-31 ESV, "Have you not known? Have you not heard? The Lord is the everlasting God, the Creator of the ends of the earth. He does not faint or grow weary; his understanding is unsearchable. He gives power to the faint, and to him who has no might he increases strength. Even youths shall faint and be weary, and young men shall fall exhausted; but they who wait for the Lord shall renew their strength; they shall mount up with wings like eagles; they shall run and not be weary; they shall walk and not faint."*

I would rather God tell me about my heart, my weaknesses and areas that need improvement than for someone else to tell me. In your walk with God there will be areas that God chooses to deal with that you cannot escape. You will be forced to not just see or identify with your weaknesses, insecurities, shortcomings, faults, issues but to face them head on. God wants you to deal with them in a positive manner. It may seem painful initially but it will be well worth it in the long run.

Believe it or not, facing your problems is something you will benefit from immensely. Pushing your flaws to the back burner prolongs issues and growth. Because God wants what's best for you, there are some things He deals with immediately, and others He gradually brings up. The bottom line is you have to address them as He is ready.

Who likes to talk about their weaknesses? Who likes to talk about areas that have been covered up, shielded, hidden, and kept out of the public's eye? No time is ever the right time; no time feels good or adequate. Yet God will choose the time and tell you, "Yes you will deal with it today. You will learn today how to overcome."

Remember, if you could overcome it alone, it would no longer be a weakness. But whether you call it a weakness or thorn, it is there until you and God get together and address it. God will provide you with an answer to when that weakness or thorn can be or will be released from your life.

I have come to the realization that I have many weaknesses. I don't like any of them. They cause me to feel inadequate at times, helpless other times and annoyed most times. They try to stifle the creativity in me. They attempt to keep me bound from my full potential. Yet with them, I maintain a level of humility always. **Luke 14:11 ESV** says, **"For everyone who exalts himself will be humbled, and he who humbles himself will be exalted."** Whatever it takes to ensure my attitude is correct and actions are proper is fine with me.

Managing strengths and weaknesses appropriately is partially what it means when scripture says in **Romans 8:28 KJV, "And we know that all things work together for good to them that love God, to them who are the called according to his purpose."** Your strengths do what they are supposed to do, and your weaknesses line up according to God's Word. Together they keep you rooted and grounded.

My strengths and my weaknesses help to shape me into who I am. **Romans 15:4 ESV** says, **"For whatever was written in former days was written for our instruction that through endurance and through the encouragement of the Scriptures we might have hope."** Jesus took on the troubles of the troubled. He jumped right in and helped those through weaknesses. Your weaknesses can assist in projecting a stronger you if you allow God to work with you and in you.

When you are open for God to deal directly with your heart, it goes from a weak or sick heart to a healthy and strong heart. So much can come from heart cleansing:

Learning to be assertive opposed to aggressive;

Learning to be impactful opposed to being closed mouthed;

Learning to dismantle darkness instead of riding the waves in silence;

Learning to disburse wisdom under any circumstance;

Learning to not become so easily offended;

Learning value even when others seek to devalue you;

Learning to stop expecting others to do what I do or to be as I am;

Realizing that choosing battles does not mean that I will be the one who gets to choose; Learning it is okay to stand alone in some instances.

Though you are never alone, one of the hardest things in the world is to feel totally alone. These feelings have the capacity to open the door to things that don't belong to you. Questioning your abilities and inabilities are common in this atmosphere because it breeds uncertainty.

Because there are so many human standards, you have to monitor closely your perspective, trusting God's instructions to you opposed to man's views. Be careful that while you're operating in what God has told you to do, if those standards don't line up with man's standards, that you don't consider yourself a failure. By God's standards, the most important standards are that you have been obedient to follow His leading. Fortunately, God has placed you on this journey and though you have not mastered the things according to man, you have sacrificed and operated out of obedience because of God.

I heard Joel Osteen say, "Sometimes in life you have to play in pain." Don't let injuries, hurt, disappointment or attacks cause you to sit on the sideline. Don't get out the game. Don't sit on the sideline nursing your wounds.

Continue being faithful to God in the tough times. Don't quit on God, and go out in silence. Hold fast to what you believed before, whatever wrong was done to you. God hasn't changed. He has not changed His mind or how He sees you. He still wants to work through you, but how will you handle the abuse, the wounds, the undeserved pain, the wrong that was done to you?

Some things come because your faith needs to go to a higher level. It needs to be stretched, and you need to see God on a higher scale than you currently know Him on. You may be hurting but stay in the game. Winners are those who didn't give up. Conquerors are those who refused to be defeated. Don't get bitter.

The Heart does Not Lie . . .

> ➢ *Proverbs 4:23 NIV, "Above all else, guard your heart, for it is the wellspring of life."*

It's easy to love God and agree with His decisions especially when they don't affect you. At any rate, knowing that God is sovereign which means He can do whatever He wants to, whenever He wants to, and however He wants to means He doesn't have to check in with us. Nor does He have to brief us on His actions, or decisions. His conclusion to a matter does not even have to make sense to us.

It is important to maintain consistency in our relationship with God. Whether He does something we like or don't like, the matter starts and ends with God. Some people know the danger in displaying bitterness toward God. It may appear that everything is fine between them and God and then a crisis comes. They may testify of His goodness and tell how He is with them, strengthening them daily to get through the crisis, but, "Wait for it." To those onlookers, there are no traces of anger, bitterness or resentment. They give continuous praise, but, "Wait for it."

Job said, **"Though you slay me, yet will I trust you." (Job 13:15)** Satan attacked Job's character, and his health. Job lost his property, and his ten children. Yet his trust remained in God. Some people have no problem trusting when it does not cost them anything. Pastor Donnie McClurkin sings, "I'll Trust You Lord." He asked a lot of faith questions in that song, "Can you still believe in Me when your life's a living hell? When all the things around you seem to quickly fade away, will you trust Me?"

We can say anything before tragedy strikes, but what will we say after the calamity? When there is dire distress resulting from loss or tragedy brought on by no fault of your own, outside of God choosing to get glory out of your life, will your words continue to be, "Though you slay me, yet will I trust you?" Or will you become bitter thinking no one can see or feel the effects of your bitterness.

Though it seems like the relationship between them and God is still in tack, the crisis has really caused them to redirect their anger. They are wise enough to know they cannot risk being upset with God, so they channel those feelings outwardly, inflicting pain on others as a means of coping with the pain.

Bitterness can eat away at the foundation of any heart if it is not dealt with properly. People begin to turn that bitterness on others and backstab, cut with their tongue or take jabs at the character of others because of their pain. They feel they are safe as long as they are not angry with God due to the devastations that occurred in their lives. But it is still wrong to inflict your hurt on innocent people who had nothing to do with what happened to you or in your life. Your negative actions still reach God although you redirected your feelings away from Him.

When a tragedy occurs in your life and God chooses to allow it to end in a manner that hurts you to the core, you cannot be okay with God, then turn on others in subtle ways and think God isn't going to notice. And because He is God, when the person you turn on is wounded or hurt because you were hurt, God gives them discernment to know that the hurt you felt was a result of you not being happy with His decision.

The moral of the story is when life tries to knock you down, be sure you don't respond by trying to knock someone else down who had nothing to do with you getting knocked down. When you lash out on others, you will be dealt with, if not by them, certainly by God. Targeting someone else, or divulging their personal information because you are hurting is wrong, deceitful, manipulative, and conniving.

Ask God to help you deal with your emotions, hurt and pain so that you don't impose them or project them on innocent people. You should not want others to hurt because you are hurting. You should not wish that on anyone. It is your cross to bear and though you think you don't deserve your cross, you cannot make anyone share your cross. Be careful when misjudging people who you think may have it better than you or may have gone through less than you.

Channeling your frustrations during affliction is a necessity. **Proverbs 16:28 MSG** says, **"Troublemakers start fights; gossips break up friendships."** I confided in a person of the cloth who was hurting due to very public but personal problem. I later discovered this person was wrestling with misplaced anger. As a result, my trust was betrayed. What I shared in confidence was openly shared.

The hurtful thing was not so much that the details of two major personal issues were shared; it was the fact that I had not done anything to warrant the betrayal. The betrayal was not simply a discussion about my personal concerns, but about the dislike this person had for me as well. It also stirred up strife that I could not afford to enter into. It was not my nature in high school and certainly not as clergy.

This incident was disturbing because as clergy, I trusted the person. I was a friend, so I thought. Some people may not be able to recognize a true friend, but I cherish the few I have. You know those people who will keep your secrets until they get angry with you, or until they get angry with the hand life deals them. Hindsight says if I had just maintained my silence a little longer instead of confiding in this person, I would not be going through this. On the other hand, I needed to talk to someone who could relate and this person was available.

As I reflected on the things said about me, I also reflected on the advice that had been given to me early on before the betrayal that helped me at a time in need. I couldn't remain angry after I learned of the betrayal because of the revelation God gave me. I pitied this person, and prayed even more because of the crisis. I tried to be a genuine friend and co-laborer, but pain pushed me away.

There's a saying, "hurt people, hurt people." There's a lot of truth to that, but I will determine in my heart not to hurt others simply because I am hurting. I strive to help others when I am hurting. Somehow it makes me feel better. I dusted myself off, and continued to run the race set before me. One thing I hold dear is the good this person did for me could not be undone after the bad. So I still win. The person talked about my issues but didn't share the fact that there was valuable advice given to me that I benefitted from.

Whether you are manipulative, conniving, sneaky or vindictive, God knows, and He knows why. A minister discovered her teenage daughter was pregnant, and from the looks of it she assumed others would judge her. Because of her own embarrassment, while she shared with other ministers that her daughter was pregnant, she dragged in personal information about another minister who had gone through the same thing with her daughter not many years before.

What that said to me was some people sling dirt when problems knock at their door. Just because you suffer a tragedy or some family problem, it does not give you the right to put another person's life on blast. Some people feel if they have to hurt, then so will others. If they are judged, they will throw others in the spotlight to be judged as well.

Undeniable Healing . . .

> *Exodus 15:26 NIV He said, "If you listen carefully to the LORD your God and do what is right in his eyes, if you pay attention to his commands and keep all his decrees, I will not bring on you any of the diseases I brought on the Egyptians, for I am the LORD, who heals you."*

Have you ever gone through something that was so devastating that as a result you received cuts, and scars, bruises and wounds? Your mind could have easily snapped but by the Grace of God. He hid you, shielded you and caused you to remain sane. Some attacks will leave you in need of desperate healing for your very mind. But my advice to you is, "Don't allow your heart to cause your mind to snap."

There are many gospel artists that sing about the fact that they could have lost their minds. One even said the devil attacked his mind with a breakdown. The mind is a person's attention or intellect.

According to Oxford Dictionaries, "It is the element of a person that enables them to be aware of the world and their experiences, to think, and to feel; the faculty of consciousness and thought."

The mind is fragile, but God holds the strains that regulate the volatile mixture of emotional and logical thinking processes. We accumulate thoughts daily. Our soul is what gives us our personality and it's through our soul that we live out our relationship with God, with other people and with ourselves.

Our soul consists of the mind, will and emotions. Our mind has a conscious part and a subconscious part. The conscious mind is where we do our thinking and reasoning. The sub-conscious mind is where we hold our deep beliefs and our attitudes. It's also where we have our feeling, our emotions and retain our memories. Our will is what gives us the ability to make choices. The mind and body communicate constantly. What the mind thinks, perceives, and experiences is sent from our brain to the rest of the body. If the mind is weak and malfunctioning, sooner or later the body will follow suit.

Sometimes our minds are overloaded. It is important to declutter the mind from all of the cares of the world. Your mind should not continuously race day in and day out from one problem to the next. Nor should you allow your thoughts to take up residence in negative spaces.

I was in a good place mentally, but I was agitated because I had an assignment that was taking me entirely too long to complete. Be specific in what you ask for. I asked God for one month off work with pay so that I could complete my book, "Finding the Common Ground: Marriage vs. Divorce." In my mind, I just wanted and needed to finish the book. I didn't care much about the details of what God would shift around to accommodate me. Nor did I consider what God would do to allow me the time. All I knew was I had a God given goal that I was driven to see accomplished and soon.

I anticipated God saying yes. But I did not calculate what that yes would actually cost me. Never in my mind did I think that along with being granted the time, I would also have a visit with affliction. I won't go into the details of it here, but I will share that the side effects of the affliction put me in bed an entire month. I had elevated blood pressure and a few more issues.

Since I was in bed anyway and slept very little, I chose to use the time to do what I asked God to give me the time for, "Finishing the book." Little did I know this book would help to keep my mind focused on the assignment opposed to where my emotions were attempting to take me. I was headed towards a breakdown. If we are not careful, the cares of the world will consume us.

Though the month off was accompanied by unwarranted abuse and unwanted stress, I did not allow my situation to shut me down. I fought to close my mind to the affliction, and focused on the assignment at hand. It's not good to run from your problems or to suppress them, but in my case, the problems were too much to deal with all at once. I dealt with them as God brought them up.

I had to fight to keep my head above water and remain focused on the positive. There were moments where, due to the stress, my brain literally went blank, blocking out periods lasting seconds at a time in mid-sentence. When I drove I either got turned around, or lost. As distracted as I felt at times, what helped me was staying in the Word.

God definitely took care of my mind. He protected me while showing me how easy it is to trip over to the other side. Thankfully, I had the chance to see the other side without vacationing there or moving there permanently. Healing never felt better.

2 Corinthians 10:3-6 NIV says, "For though we live in the world, we do not wage war as the world does. The weapons we fight with are not the weapons of the world. On the contrary, they have divine power to demolish strongholds. We demolish arguments and every pretension that sets itself up against the knowledge of God, and we take captive every thought to make it obedient to Christ. And we will be ready to punish every act of disobedience, once your obedience is complete." I had to put every negative thought under arrest. The truth was I believed every word that proceeded from the mouth of God, not my feelings or what things looked like.

If you shut down the negative thought immediately, it cannot take root. If it does not take root, it will not form as a stronghold.

Replace all impure thoughts with pure thoughts. Don't allow random thoughts to invade you, or to override your good. Instead, think on things that are pure. Paul said in **Philippians 4:8 NLT, "And now, dear brothers and sisters, one final thing. Fix your thoughts on what is true, and honorable, and right, and pure, and lovely, and admirable. Think about things that are excellent and worthy of praise."** If it's not positive, kick it out. You cannot afford to hang out with negative thoughts. They are not worth the risk.

Victimization . . .

> ➢ *1 Peter 2:18-21 KJV, "Slaves, in reverent fear of God submit yourselves to your masters, not only to those who are good and considerate, but also to those who are harsh. For it is commendable if someone bears up under the pain of unjust suffering because they are conscious of God. But how is it to your credit if you receive a beating for doing wrong and endure it? But if you suffer for doing good and you endure it, this is commendable before God. To this you were called, because Christ suffered for you, leaving you an example that you should follow in his steps."*

Victims are often victimized over and over, first at the hands of the offender, then through the ignorance of others. Instead of helping the person affected, some people rather reach out with sympathy to the person that caused the harm. They show leniency toward the offender and neglect the wrong the victim has suffered. Some feel the victim should be strong enough to recover or should have been strong enough to not allow the offense to harm them from the start.

They want you to be merciful towards the person ignoring or down playing what you endured. The bottom line is the victim does not deserve under any circumstances to be re-victimized. The victim's character should not end up on trial. They should not have to defend their name.

Everyone needs a support system. God has given me my own positive circle of supporters to get me through rough times. These people range from encouragers, intercessors, cheerleaders, mentors to coaches and they have tremendous access to wisdom, God's ear and His heart. Who are they? Of course you want to know. This is the private circle, though there are others outside the circle that are blessings too.

I call on them at any given moment and without asking; get exactly what I need from each of them. You should compile a circle of your own. Do not invite toxic minds to join in. You need a safe place to clear your head and talk openly. Make those you allow in your circle qualify. You should have a track record with them, tested, tried and true.

People will abandon you for whatever reasons. It's something how people who have nothing to do with your affliction will stop speaking to you when you go through. Some people despise others for standing up for themselves. They will go to great lengths to place negative labels on you upon learning that you spoke to an injustice. Others run from you afraid you will ask them to tell what they know or witnessed. In cases like this, it's necessary to surround yourself with people who actually know you and love you.

Outside of my circle I have my writing. Thankfully for me, every book I write is rooted in the Word. It does not matter the subject, it still comes back to God, what He says, what He did and what He is going to do. I do not want to give my issues my full attention so I continue to feed my spirit. I could not have made it out of any past battles without bathing myself in the Word of God. I call it, "Sitting at the Feet of Jesus."

Albertina Walker and the Caravans sing in her song, "In Times like These," "Be very sure your anchor holds and grip a solid rock. That rock is Jesus." I hide under the shadow of His wings in the spirit realm but I hide in my writing when things get hectic. I go into this trance of writing and find solace there. I don't want to come out. I feel justified because writing is something God has allowed me to do. It's one of my gifts. But I also recognize it is my escape.

When I don't want to deal with a thing, but I want to do something constructive that keeps me tapped into my relationship with God, that's my go to. It's my outlet. So I run, but not to some source or vice that would harm me. Though it is not harmful, it allows me to preoccupy my mind or self-medicate until the issue is over. Or at least until I can or am ready to deal with it. It's how I, in my own strength, stay sane. Now, the right way would be to deal with the issues head on, but that was not how I operated. It wasn't until God put the brakes on and let me know that dealing with issues head on was what He wired me to do. I had to step up to the plate.

My husband even noted, "Every time you go through a crisis you write a book." I know what he meant by that, but it also meant that I did not resort to destructive or unhealthy things in a crisis. I have learned writing is fine, a great sense of therapy, but not a replacement for handling issues.

Healing happens in atmospheres of freedom. I am free in my mind to speak my heart and confront issues. With all I experienced and all of the pressures and stress I was subjected to, I survived. With all I have gone through, if those things were the worst that could be done to me, then I am a mighty warrior who by God's Grace, Might and Power crossed over in victory.

Whether we are chosen as victims or thrown into pits, God takes every wrong and makes it right. He restores in ways unimaginable. Though I have been the victim of much, I will never be helpless. I will rise above every unjust act, operating in the fullness of the authority given me before birth. You bring God glory in how you handle what you endure. How you go in isn't what's important, it's how you come out of it.

My Response to the Heart . . .

> ➤ *Jeremiah 17:9-10 NIV, "The heart is deceitful above all things and beyond cure. Who can understand it? "I the Lord search the heart and examine the mind, to reward each person according to their conduct, according to what their deeds deserve."*

The heart is deceitful. That sounds horrible considering it is located within my body. Yet if we are not watchful the heart will mislead us. The message translation of **Jeremiah 17:9-10** says, **"The heart is hopelessly dark and deceitful, a puzzle that no one can figure out. But I, GOD, search the heart and examine the mind. I get to the heart of the human. I get to the root of things. I treat them as they really are, not as they pretend to be."**

You can go from being a positive and compassionate person to becoming cold and uncaring. David said in **Psalm 73:26 NIV, "My flesh and my heart may fail, but God is the strength of my heart and my portion forever."** Therefore I put my trust in God and not in my heart. My heart has allowed me to ache over much and become down-trodden at times, but God has elevated me far above my heart.

Problems are inevitable in all of our lives, but we have to mindful of how we respond to them. I work hard at not allowing ill feelings to enter in. I cannot afford the consequences that go along with having a deceitful heart.

Learning to replace every impure thought with a declaration takes time but is worth every second. I remember the doctor saying to me as he read my EKG, the machine showed I had a heart attack, but it was in error. Yet he followed up by sending me to the emergency room to be retested. After three tests, I did not have a heart attack. However, I learned that stress was masquerading as a heart attack.

Upon leaving the ER I was sent for a stress test. I declared a healthy heart. The doctor confirmed I did not have a sick heart. His words were true because I gave my heart to God many years ago. **Proverbs 23:26 KJV** says, **"My son, give me thine heart, and let thine eyes observe my ways."** Because I desire to know God and to please Him my heart is open to Him.

I knew my heart was healthy. I knew the blood causing my heart to pump came straight from Jesus. I have been redeemed, washed in the blood of the lamb. The doctor went on to say I had the heart of a young person in their thirties. Though I was in my late forties, I received that too. My heart was restored as unto my youth. God purified it.

I am not perfect by a long shot, but I have been told by many that I have a good heart. While that is indeed true, I know what it is when your heart creeps over to the other side. It's certainly not a good place. I learned you can fuel the heart with what you want and it will accept it. If you meditate on evil, the heart will provide you with accommodation, just as if you meditate on righteousness, the heart will reasonably accommodate you.

Everything you do flows from your heart, whether good or bad. **(Proverbs 4:23 NIV)** That's why it is important to guard your heart. I don't like the ways of many, but I refused to succumb to their standards. It is not optional for me to not forgive. I don't have the luxury of harboring bitter feelings for even a season. Whatever I do affects me. I am held accountable in the strictest way.

I don't ever want to attempt manipulation to appease my flesh. I would rather have God smile when He mentions my name than frown. I care about what He thinks about me. He is my heart regulator.

Conclusion . . .

I have discovered that everyone has a path on this journey. Some follow as closely as they know how. Others make it difficult. Whether you feel stuck or think you're advancing the way you need to, the journey continues. The only way to live the healthiest life possible is by obeying God, and accepting and following the plan He has laid out for you.

The journey consists of a route, detours, and proper connections, and may come with distractions. Whether you are doing something you enjoy or tolerate, God uses it all for His glory. God also uses whatever route necessary to get you where you need to be on time. The route He maps out is needed for so many intricate details to come together.

When you recognize that everyone is essential to the kingdom of God, and all play a major and significant role, you will begin to see how everything links together. We are each a piece of the puzzle. We intricately fit together neatly, as God intended.

Fortunately, we have the Hope of Glory at our disposal as we seek to follow the travel itinerary closely. The path we are expected to follow will sometimes be narrow or even seem broad, but God provides opportunities for learning for us all.

The learning curve along the journey is necessary as God provides us with teachable moments. His will is that we prosper. The heart of God is toward His children. He desires that we be in good health in every aspect of the word healthy, spiritually and naturally.

God makes provision for us. He gives us everything we need to be successful. He doesn't hide anything from us. He makes clear the plans He has for each of us. Not only does He give revelation and guidance, but He gives visions and dreams which are encompassed in the call. These visions and dreams provide a visual and give clarity to help you navigate through life with the most accuracy and impact. It gives insight into some of what God is doing in people in the earth realm.

The journey does not come without its challenges and difficulties. But with every assignment, God is faithful to see you through to completion. When you are alert to God's timing, He will not slack in showing you the effectiveness of your assignment. He teaches you how to maneuver through darkness and get over every hurdle. Then He allows you to walk in the victory because of all He has done. Just as you celebrate the victories, God celebrates and He rejoices over you.

The call is incorporated in the plan. It defines where God is taking you and how He wants you to spend your days on earth. Your destiny was preplanned and well thought out long ago. Don't despise your cross. Embrace it, knowing full well that God gave you the right cross. He gave you the one He knew you could handle. He designed you specifically for it.

Authenticity goes a long way and makes for an easier journey. Being your authentic self is effortless. You will be well able to accomplish the things set out by God when you are true to who you are. God will even expand your assignment when He sees that you are confident in the "you" He created.

Transition will occur as God increases in you. You will go from levels to dimensions. Elevation will be rapid in some areas and appear at a standstill in other areas. Know that God will protect you at any cost, and He goes to great lengths to ensure you exceed and excel in the things He calls you to.

God gives you what you need and takes away what you don't need. It may not necessarily be obvious to you, but what you don't need will always be to your detriment. Whether God provides through addition or subtraction, He has your best interest and can see further than you can.

Wisdom teaches us to prepare for every moment. Sometimes we are so busy "doing" that we don't have time to perfect what we are doing. God will utilize us, bringing forth all He has deposited in us. Our responsibility is to be ready, making sure we use what we have effectively.

Understanding the call on your life is of equal importance in understanding the importance of bringing God glory with that call.

When you are doing what you were created to do, fulfillment will be ever present. Godly contentment is a luxury. The peace of God will surely rest upon you when you are on one accord with God.

You may be satisfied with where your walk has led you, or dissatisfied. Regardless to what side you find yourself on, the journey continues. Because people will always be involved along the journey, the heart will always be at risk of being compromised. However, the most critical thing to remember is, the most important thing in life is People. God uses us to impact the lives of others.

Healthy Living occurs on two levels, the natural and the spiritual. The body needs to be fit to do the real work of the Lord, and the spirit has to be willing to accomplish the things of God. You will never be truly happy and at total peace until you do what you were created to do.

What you are doing now may not be what you will do later. Just because you are taken in a new direction does not mean you are not on track. Often you will find, nothing you did was wasteful, it was all part of the bigger plan. The same plan that was originally in effect for you is still in effect.

Life doesn't always make sense, but God always makes sense of your life. To a certain degree, if you belong to God, you cannot stray too far from that plan. When you're really walking with God, everything is not going to make sense. It's a faith journey.

When we surrender to God trusting that He knows exactly what He is doing, our trust in Him only deepens. Tune your ears and turn your heart towards God and watch Him work before your very eyes. He turns your weaknesses into strengths, and highlights your strengths.

When God does heart transformations, undeniable healing occurs. He restores every area, leaving nothing undone. This journey we are on has benefits, fringe benefits might I add. Until you reach your divine place in God, do what you know to do with what you have and where you are. God will not leave you information-less when you follow through on the thing He gives you. He is looking for obedience, which says, take heed to His instruction.

A journey to healthy living is a process. It results in true freedom. He who the Son sets free is free indeed. The journey on earth won't conclude until we leave earth, but we ought to travel first class. The abundant life is the desired goal on earth. Life everlasting is the prize after earth. God designed earth and heaven, making complete wholeness attainable for us now and later.

Jesus' journey was our ultimate blueprint for life. He demonstrated life, showing us how to walk along earth, and through the valley of the shadow of death. He exercised His full authority and dominion on earth and in hell. He conquered death and the grave, and talked to them, "death where is your sting?"

Resurrection showed us how to get up from dead situations, not being held in bondage to anyone or anything. As you continue to embark upon the true journey destined for you, I pray you will experience the vastness of God's Glory. His treasures are forevermore.

Teresa is also the Author of five additional books:

How to Die and Stay Dead

We all need to deny ourselves of all unrighteousness. This testimony captures how to live a life pleasing to God. It shows how to do God's will and live heavenly in a worldly environment. Apply these truths and applications to your life and minimize the drama. Seek a permanent change. Don't settle for things that are temporal. Peace of mind is priceless, and it is part of your reward.

Deny your flesh. Get to the point where you're tired of crying, hurting, complaining, and being angry and unfulfilled. Enough is enough! Don't continue in your mess any longer. Life isn't always fair. But doing things your way or the world's way is a no-win situation. Life's experiences, lessons, challenges, setbacks, and issues all work together. All things work together for our good. No area is irrelevant with God.

Principles of Denying the Flesh

The purpose of this book is to reach churches, ministries, outreach groups, book clubs, study groups and the general public, providing a tool to assist individuals in living as ordained by God. This book, coupled with "How to Die and Stay Dead" goes to great lengths, lays out analogies, and provides guidance. If you are ready to go to another dimension in God, this book is for you.

The Land Flowing with Milk and Honey

One of the most frightening things is missing out on all God has for me. God has an inheritance for each of us. It's rightfully ours, but like a will, oftentimes there are prerequisites to receiving the full inheritance. The Land Flowing with Milk and Honey has been set aside for us. With proper instruction and guidance, I believe we can go in and possess the Land. Don't forfeit your inheritance!

Treasures of Hope: Testimonies of Hope

We all have treasures within. When we explore those treasures, "we offer hope to a dying world." Treasures of hope will release so many others to share their experiences without guilt, shame or condemnation. Even the soft spoken will begin to allow their stories to burst forth like thunder. In order to become an overcomer, deliverance of some sort has to take place. We have each been given a gift, not a gift of gab, but a gift of the word of our testimony. When we use our testimonies to glorify God, we show others that, though there will always be "tests," the "monies" are never too far behind. Move outside of yourself and inspire others to live. Come out of bondage to secrecy.

Finding the Common Ground: Marriage vs Divorce

Loaded with tasteful humor tailored to fit and soothe the ache of heart-wrenching situations, this book will help you to resuscitate your marriage. Tender subjects are visited and dealt with in a pragmatic way that will bring life to dead situations. The tips and advice packed within the pages of this small book will force you to rethink divorce and separation, as well as begin a new journey to wholeness. After all, marriage is for the mature of heart.

Notes

Chapter One

Sandy Warner: God speaks through different kinds of Visions, www.thequickenedword.com

Scriptural References

Chapter One: The Plan

Jeremiah 6:16 NLT

John 14:1-6 KJV

Philippians 2:13 NIV

Ephesians 2:10 NLT

Jeremiah 29:11 NIV

Philippians 4:6 NIV

Habakkuk 2:2-3 NLT

Matthew 6:33 NLT

1 Corinthians 11:1 NIV

Chapter One: The Detour

Exodus 13:17-18 NLT

Proverbs 16:9 NLT

Joshua 5:6 NLT

Chapter One: The Connection

1John 1:1-4 NLT

John 17:1-5 NIV

John 17:6-12 NIV

Dr. Teresa S. Johnson

John 17:13-19 NIV

John 17:24-26 NIV

Psalm 119:50 NIV

Isaiah 49:16 ESV

John 3:17 AMP

John 3:19-20 AMP

Chapter One: The Sideshow Distractions

1 Corinthians 7:35 NLT

Proverbs 4:25-27 MSG

John 3:21 AMP

Hebrews 4:15 NIV

Matthew 4:1-11 MSG

John 10:10 NIV

Proverbs 16:3 NLT

Romans 8:14-15 ESV

Philippians 4:8 KJV

Chapter One: The Hope of Glory

Colossians 1:27 NLT

Psalm 37:5-6 ESV

John 15:1-4 ESV

Psalm 18:32 NIV

Proverbs 12:15 NIV

Proverbs 15:22 NIV

Psalm 32:8-11 ESV

Psalm 37:23 NIV

James 4:17 ESV

Romans 6:23 NIV

Psalm 139:1-4 NLT

Chapter One: The Travel Itinerary

Proverbs 3:23 MSG

Romans 12:2 ESV

John 2:15-16 ESV

Isaiah 32:17 NIV

Chapter One: The Path

Proverbs 4:26 ESV

Hebrews 5:4 AMP

Hebrews 5:9 AMP

Acts 9

John 6:51 KJV

John 6:53 ESV

1 John 5:11-13 GNT

Chapter One: The Learning Curve

1Timothy 2:1-6 ESV

Chapter One: The Heart of God

1 John 3:1-3 ESV

Hebrews 3:7-13 NIV

Hebrews 3:16-19 NIV

Psalm 27:4-5 ESV

Chapter One: My Response to the Plan

Galatians 2:20 NIV

Galatians 6:10 NIV

Proverbs 3:27 NIV

Chapter Two: Visions and Dreams

Acts 2:17-18 NIV

Chapter Two: The Clear Picture

1 Corinthians 13:12 MSG

2 Corinthians 12:1-6

Acts 16:9-10

Jude 1:23

Acts 18:9-11

Chapter Two: The Night Vision

Job 33:14-18 KJV

Proverbs 28:1 ESV

Revelation 5:5

Chapter Two: The Timing

Colossians 4:5 AMP

1 Corinthians 1:23 NIV

Chapter Two: The Dark Side

Ephesians 5:11 ESV

Ephesians 5:8 NASB

Luke 8:17 NASB

2 Corinthians 4:6 NASB

Isaiah 42:16 ESV

John 8:12 NASB

John 1:5 NLT

Revelation 12:11 KJV

Acts 26:17-18 MSG

Psalm 119:105 NIV

Chapter Two: The Assignment

1 Corinthians 7:17 NIV

John 17:18 MSG

Isaiah 49:6

2 Timothy 1:1-2 MSG

1 Corinthians 7:17 NIV

Romans 8:28 KJV

Daniel 11:32 MSG

Chapter Two: The Faithfulness of God

2 Thessalonians 3:3 NIV

Isaiah 55:11 NIV

Numbers 23:19 ESV

Deuteronomy 7:9 NIV

Genesis 18:16-32 NIV

2 Corinthians 4:8 ASV

Psalm 118:8 AMP

Psalm 92:1-4 CEV

Chapter Two: The Effective Place

2 Timothy 2:15 ESV

James 2:17 NIV

2 Corinthians 4:7 KJV

Chapter Two: The Evidence Speaks for Itself

Ephesians 3:14-20 NIV

James 5:16 NIV

Psalm 109:1-20 KJV

1 Thessalonians 5:22 AMP

1 John 3:8 MSG

Jonah 3:3-10 NIV

Psalm 4:8 ESV

Matthew 1:18-25 ESV

Chapter Two: My Response to the Visions and Dreams

Ephesians 3:7 NIV

Psalm 84:11 NLT

Ephesians 3:7-13 MSG

Chapter Three: The Importance of Your Cross

1 Corinthians 1:18 KJV

1 Peter 2:21-25 MSG

Philippians 1:6 NLT

Matthew 22:14 KJV

2 Timothy 1:9 KJV

Psalm 119:60 NIV

1 Corinthians 1:9 NLT

Romans 11:29 NLT

Chapter Three: Walking in Your Authentic Call

1 John 2:27 ESV

Luke 12:48 NIV

Ephesians 4:1 NLT

Chapter Three: Expanding the Assignment

Romans 8:30 MSG

Ephesians 2:10

1 Samuel 15:22-23 NLT

1 Samuel 15:24 NLT

John 1:1 NIV

Matthew 28:18-20 ESV

Chapter Three: In the Valley of Transition

Ecclesiastes 7:8 ESV

Genesis 9:12-17 NIV

Chapter Three: The Protected Season

Leviticus 26:4 AMP

Proverbs 18:16 NIV

Luke 17:11-19 NIV

Psalm 143:8 NASB

Zechariah 4:10 NLT

Luke 7:28 NIV

Jude 1:23 ESV

Luke 15:10 KJV

Chapter Three: When the Temporary Provision Lifts

Isaiah 43:16-19 NIV

Chapter Three: Preparation

Luke 12:35-40 ESV

Genesis 45:4-11 NIV

Chapter Three: Understanding the Call

Ephesians 4:11-12 NASB

Exodus 3:9-12 MSG

Exodus 4:1; 10-13 MSG

Amos 7:10-17 MSG

Luke 23:39-43 AMP

Psalm 32:7 NIV

Psalm 32:8 NLT

1 Corinthians 12:8-10 KJV

Matthew 5:9

Chapter Three: The Call that brings Godly Contentment

1 Corinthians 7:17 ESV

1 Thessalonians 5:18 MSG

2 Kings 7:3-5 ESV

1 Corinthians 3:7 NLT

1 Corinthians 2:9 KJV

Luke 24:45 NIV

Proverbs 3:13-18 KJV

Proverbs 3:5

Jeremiah 17:7 NLT

Chapter Three: My Response to the Call

Colossians 1:15-23 NIV

Colossians 1:15-23 MSG

Chapter Four: The Heart: A Hard Place

Zephaniah 3:17 NIV

Chapter Four: Controlling Your Emotions

Joshua 1:9 ESV

2 Corinthians 4:8-12 GNT

Chapter Four: Trust the God in You

1 John 4:4 NLT

Isaiah 55:1-5 KJV

James 1:5 NASB

Chapter Four: Deeper Levels of Trust

Proverbs 3:5-6 NLT

Ephesians 6:11-12 ESV

Ephesians 6:13-16

Ephesians 6:17

Chapter Four: Strengths verses Weaknesses

Isaiah 40:28-31 ESV

Luke 14:11 ESV

Romans 8:28 KJV

Romans 15:4 ESV

Chapter Four: The Heart does Not Lie

Proverbs 4:23 NIV

Job 13:15

Proverbs 16:28 MSG

Chapter Four: Undeniable Healing

Exodus 15:26 NIV

2 Corinthians 10:3-6 NIV

Philippians 4:8 NLT

Chapter Four: Victimization

1 Peter 2:18-21 KJV

Chapter Four: My Response to the Heart

Jeremiah 17:9-10 NIV

Psalm 73:26 NIV

Proverbs 23:26 KJV

Proverbs 4:23 NIV

Printed in the United States
By Bookmasters